Traditional Witchcraft for the Seashore

Traditional Witchcraft for the Seashore

Mélusine Draco

Winchester, UK
Washington, USA

First published by Moon Books, 2012
Moon Books is an imprint of John Hunt Publishing Ltd., Laurel House, Station Approach,
Alresford, Hants, SO24 9JH, UK
office1@o-books.net
www.o-books.com

For distributor details and how to order please visit the 'Ordering' section on our website.

Text copyright: Mélusine Draco 2010

ISBN: 978 1 84694 426 0

A CIP catalogue record for this book is available from the British Library.

Design: Lee Nash

Printed in the UK by CPI Antony Rowe
Printed in the USA by Offset Paperback Mfrs, Inc

We operate a distinctive and ethical publishing philosophy in all
areas of our business, from our global network of authors to
production and worldwide distribution.

CONTENTS

The chapter headings refer to classical music pieces taking their theme from the sea:

Sea Fever (Ireland),
Four Sea Interludes (Britten),
Sea Drift (Delius),
Sea Pictures (Elgar),
Calm Sea (Mendelssohn),
The Roaring of a Wave (Sibelius),
Toward the Sea (Takemitsu) and
Sea and Sky (Finnissy).

Nothing of him that doth fade,
But doth suffer a sea-change
Into something rich and strange.

The Tempest : William Shakespeare

Chapter One

Sea Fever

Around the world there are thousands of miles of coastline: rugged cliffs, tidal-battered rocky shores, sweeping estuaries, gentle brackish creeks, golden sand and shingle beaches. Although each has an enchantment all of its own, few of us are fortunate to live near enough to the sea to use this dramatic shoreline as a regular magical working area. And yet, for a natural witch, born and bred by the sea, the beach and rocky shore are equally as magical as the inland woods and hills of more traditional approaches to witchcraft.

Our shorelines also provide every kind of haunting landscape – from mysterious sea-caves and treacherous, misty salt-marshes; to endless beaches and rock pools; and salt-water estuaries where trees grow right down to the water's edge, and petrified forests emerge at low tide. The diverseness of our northern Atlantic coastlines in particular … from Shetland to Scilly, to Norway and Brittany, from Newfoundland to Cape Cod …owe these distinctive characteristics to constant erosion, salt spray and the battering of spring and winter gales. The sea carves rocks into jagged cliffs and smoothes the sand of a beach – but even if there is no shortage of breathtaking scenery in which to create a sacred space, it is the *sea* itself that provides the real focus for our magical energies.

Step back for a moment into those distant childhood memories and visualise a day at the seaside – but strip away the images of crowded tourist beaches and focus on the *sound of the movement* of the sea. If you need any reminder, hold a large seashell to your ear and summon up the voice of the waves. In the depths of our subconscious mind this sound will be a low, muted purr as small waves lap at the water margin; or the roaring of breakers against a sea wall; or the sly, insidious murmur as the tide begins to turn along narrow channels and between sand banks. In fact, we can never encounter the sea in any of its moods, without being aware of its movement; the waves on its surface and the tides and currents, which send it swirling around the globe.

And even if we never went near the sea except for an annual summer holiday, most of us from Scandinavia, and around the British and Irish coasts to Iceland, can instantly recall the sonorous, chant of the daily shipping forecast that took us on a flight of fancy to the wildest coastlines around our shores. Broadcast four times a day, the radio brought us a brief moment of sea-magic, as wonderful and evocative as a Latin Mass ...

Viking : North Utsire : South Utsire : Forties : Fisher : Cromarty Forth : Tyne : Dogger : German Bight : Humber : Thames : Dover : Wight : Portland : Plymouth : Biscay : Trafalgar : FitzRoy : Sole : Lunday : Irish Sea : Fastnet : Shannon : Rockall : Malin : Hebrides : Bailey : Fair Isle : Faeroes : South East Iceland ...

This mysterious, but totally meaningless jumble of words, still has the ability to conjure up pictures of grey, heaving northern seas with lashing rain and gale force winds. By stark contrast, it also has the ability to evoke warm, family memories of childhood tea-tables, cosy firesides, and comfort food – although perhaps not for those who were being warned that a gale force-nine was headed in their direction.

This brief maritime detour is included to demonstrate how potent simple words can be; how a rhythmic recital can paint mind pictures in much the same way that an evocative piece of music can. And even if the US marine forecast doesn't produce quite the same kind of enchantment, Fleetwood Mac's *Albatross*, can summon images of this magnificent bird gliding effortlessly over the waves, a tireless companion of sailors in the southern seas.

This is the first lesson in sea magic ...

The sea (or ocean) covers about 70% of the earth's surface and at its deepest goes down some 30,000+ feet through a vast underwater landscape of submarine canyons, submerged mountain ranges and steep-sided rock pillars, whose volcanic tips form the oceanic islands. The deepest spot in the Atlantic Ocean lies off Hispaniola in the Caribbean; while the world's greatest ocean depth is in the Mariana Trench, south of Japan.

Around the land-mass, the sea-floor slopes away forming a 'continental shelf', which can vary greatly in width; from just a few miles off the west coast of much of the Americas, up to 560 miles of the coast of Siberia. In places, this shelf is gouged with deep grooves of those original river valleys, called *rias*, where land has become submerged beneath the encroaching sea. Like the lower Hudson Valley, and that whole section of American eastern coastline, that was drowned by the sea at the end of the last Ice Age, leaving a submarine canyon about 110 miles long.

Geological upheavals of the past have determined entire landscapes in a 'relentless programme of erosion on the one hand and deposition on the other'. In simple terms, this refers to the fact that much of what we think of as an *inland* landscape may be made up of sheets of sedimentary rock laid down on the floor of some ancient sea, which at different times has covered the land. For example, three times in the past 180 million years, what is now called the 'lowlands' of England have lain beneath the sea; and parts of East Anglia would be below sea level today if it were not for the 50–100 feet of deposited glacial clay and gravel. Even those potential sea-witches living some distance from the present shoreline, can rest easy in the knowledge that the land on which they stand was probably once beneath the sea!

Like her inland counterparts, a sea-witch's life is still governed by natural tides and elements – although here they may seem to appear under a different guise to those of conventional rural Craft. The sea is the driving force that powers and modifies the world's climate, transporting huge quantities of solar-derived energy across the globe in the process. For those who live by the sea, Nature's tides are even more relevant to the daily routine than for those living inland ... simply because it can mean the difference between life and death if we get it wrong. The sea is the last unconquered environment on this planet and possibly the most dangerous – but that's what gives it its appeal.

Tides and seasons

Since the beginning of time, when man first stood on the shoreline and wondered at the vastness of the ocean, it has been recognised that the tides (the periodic rise and fall of great stretches of water), had something to do with the moon. Neither did it take him long to calculate that the usual interval between them was about 12½ hours; roughly half the time the moon takes to circle the earth. Nowhere else on earth was Nature's power and glory so much in evidence.

In *Sea & Seashore*, Sir Isaac Newton's words are used to explain the tides as being due to the moon's gravitational pull on the water, lifting it to form a bulge resembling an enormous wave-crest. There are in fact two such bulges, one on the side of the earth facing the moon, and the other on the earth's far side, for there the moon's pull draws the earth away from the water. Between the two bulges the water is lowered, as though in the trough between these gigantic wave-crests. The friction between the water and the rotating earth slows the movement of these bulges, so that instead of being exactly beneath the moon, they lag a little behind. For this reason, *high tide*, as the bulge is called, does not occur exactly when the moon is overhead, but somewhat later.

The sun's gravitational pull similarly raises tides akin to, but less powerful than those caused by the moon. Their period is about 12 hours instead of the 12½ - but the two interact. At full and new moon, when the sun and moon are in a straight line with the earth – this recurs at intervals of about a fortnight – they co-operate to produce an especially powerful *spring tide*. This has nothing to do with the annual season: spring tides occur throughout the year and rise higher and fall lower than usual, although the lowest spring tides of the year occur around the Spring Equinox. At the first and third quarters, when the sun and moon form a right angle with the earth (again, roughly, at fortnightly intervals) – the pull conflicts, making a *neap tide* whose range is unusually small.

This means, of course, that we need to tear ourselves away from the stereotypical 'triple moon-goddess' concept governing the lunar phases, and think more in terms of the natural interaction of *both* astrological bodies, the Sun *and* Moon, moving in a cosmic rhythm of perpetual motion – manifesting in the form of ebbing and flowing of the Earthly sea. Some may be reluctant to accept this idea but it is a scientific fact that, despite its impressive gravitational pull, the moon is a dead, barren place, reflecting the sun's light, not its own.

Although the ancients had no way of knowing all this on a scientific level, it is interesting to recall that the lunar goddesses, Artemis, Diana and Luna were sterile, barren representations that needed solar energy (Apollo/Helios/Sol) to act as a counter-balance. This is what is known magically as 'old wisdom' – the true interpretation behind the myths and legends, recorded in folk-lore and fable since time began and logged into our universal, or collective subconscious – not the modern 'fake-lore' currently in vogue. Without coming to grips with this ancient 'science', our own modern magic will become sterile and stunted.

So, let us return to the sea …in mid ocean, the tides, like ordinary waves, are simply a rhythmic rise and fall of the water. On the continental shelf, however, they act like the waves on a beach, and become a bodily rush of the water towards, or away from the land. The rising water produces the tide's flow or flood; its fall is the ebb, and between them, when the tide is almost at a standstill, there are brief periods of slack water. This rise and fall takes place twice every day, but high or low tides occur about 50½ minutes later each day *and alter drastically throughout the month*. While most shores have two high tides every day, some have only one, and some none at all.

Instead of one great progressive tide circling the earth, there are a number of *local* tides, differing greatly in the areas they cover, and the sea-witch recognises the importance of knowing about them from both a magical and safety point of view. Besides the familiar tides of the *ocean-tides*, there are also two other examples to take into account: *earth-tides* and *atmospheric-tides*. Earth-tides refer to the alternating slight change of shape of the Earth due to the gravitational action of the sun and moon, and atmospheric tides of the alternating slight motions of the atmosphere, which have the same cause and effect. The moon draws away the envelope of air that surrounds the Earth to produce the regular daily atmospheric tides.

Joint research by a team from the Ordnance Survey at Newcastle University and the Proudman Oceanographic Laboratory at Birkenhead has revealed more evidence of the effects of these earth-tides. The results show that parts of western Britain and Ireland, for example, 'bounce' by four inches and that the movement is caused as tides ebb and flow twice daily! The nationwide survey also showed that the deformation of the Earth's crust varies across the country and that the eastern side is much more stable than the west.

According to a spokesman for the project, when the tide is in, the extra weight of the water on the continental shelf pushes the adjoining crust down a few inches. At low tide, the Earth springs back. 'Because tidal ranges are greater on the south-western side of the British Isles, that is where the biggest bounce can be found.' The western tip of England, west Wales, the Western Isles and southern Ireland, have the biggest range of movements. Again, we have *scientific proof* of cosmic influences on the very earth on which we stand, so magical working can be timed to coincide with these natural movements for greater effect.

- **High tide**, just before the water pressure is at its greatest, would be the best time for positive or drawing magic.

- **Low tide**, when the tide has turned and the earth is about to 'bounce' back, is the time for banishing or reducing magic.

Calendars and almanacs give the dates of the moon's phases (which should be part of every witch's magical observances), but for the sea-witch it is essential to also consult local tide tables (usually given in local newspapers) so that we always know the actual times of high and low tide for our area. For example, if high tide takes place today at 4.43am and again at 4.41pm, then low tide will occur about half-way between, say around 10.40am. Magical synchronicity is the secret key-word.

If these ideas still seems far-fetched, let us reminder ourselves of the research carried out on oysters transported from their 'home' to a distant location. In laboratory tanks the oysters still displayed a marked tidal rhythm, opening their shells to feed at high tide, and closing at the ebb at their former home on Long Island Sound. During the first days of their move, the pattern in the tank remained the same; but after two weeks, the oysters were no longer opening and closing in harmony with the tide that washed their distant 'home' but now opened up at the time the tide *would have been locally* … had the town been on a sea shore, and not perched on the bank of Lake Michigan, some 580 feet above sea level!

If a simple organism like an oyster living away from the ocean can be instinctively influenced by natural tides, then the saying: 'Time and tide wait for no man,' should be writ large in every sea-witch's magical diary. This is because we will be learning how to synchronise our own psychic/magical energy with those natural tidal forces, and to discover that many old superstitions and beliefs often conceal truths, or half-truths, based on sound observation. Even if we live some distance from the sea.

Where sea and river meet

There are other powerful tidal energy points of which we should be aware, and these occur where the outward flowing river (fresh water) meets the incoming sea (salt water). The larger estuaries have attracted vast tracts of urban development and shipping industries but the smaller ones, which are of more interest to the sea-witch, are often just a small river or stream flowing into the sea. Many of them can trace their origins back to the end of the last Ice Age, when the deep river-valleys were flooded about 10,000 years ago.

Whether the estuary is formed from a deep gorge, or from wide, flooded lowlands, there is always a region where sea and river meet; where fresh and salt water moves up and down with the tide. Within a sheltered estuary there are rarely waves but this calm is deceiving: on the Hudson River tidal influences extend as far inland as Albany, where there is a 4-5 foot high tide. The level of the water is constantly fluctuating with the tidal inflow and the fresh water outflow, which increases after heavy rain. Here there are the added dangers of swift currents that are so powerful they can rip trees from the banks when the river is in flood.

Out in the estuary the water is layered: fresh water at the surface flowing seaward, heavier salt water at the bottom, which flows upstream with the tide; and in between brackish water – a mixture of river water and sea water – moving in either direction according to the ebb and flow. Creatures living in this environment must be able to survive the constantly changing salinity brought about by tidal fluctuation.

- Where fresh and seawater meet, is the perfect place to cast spells of confusion and chaos. Throw an unobtrusive plastic container (a small medicine bottle with the label removed is perfect) containing your charm into the tide and let the natural currents carry it where they will.

- There is no way of retrieving this charm, so no knee-jerk reactions when making the decision to cast it. If it *does* come back to you on the returning tide, then you *must* retrieve it and destroy the contents, since the 'powers that be' have rejected your appeal.

- Remember that retrieval could be extremely dangerous, so ensure that your reasons for casting the charm in the first place have sufficient justification, or there could be serious repercussions, and you'll only have yourself to blame.

This hostile environment of the estuary, however, is also a place of re-birth. Tidal mudbanks or mudflats begin to form from sediment brought in by the tide from the seabed, and washed downstream by the rivers. On a grand scale, along its lower course, the Mississippi carries about half a billion tonnes of sediment to the sea each year and the delta has shifted over an area of about 200 square miles during the last 6,000 years. Similarly, the Gulf of California once extended much further north until the Colorado River changed its course in prehistoric times. Sediment deposited on the river's banks dammed the Gulf, creating the current coastline and the great Salton Sink, a stretch of former seabed that extends inland some 300 miles.

As strange as it may seem, these tidal mudflats represent some of the most fertile land we have, being more 'protein-productive' than the cornfields, or the rich cattle pastures that may have contributed to their soil. This process continues over hundreds of years until the mudbank is high enough to support vegetation – at which point the 'saltmarsh succession' takes over to create solid land. Nevertheless, mudbanks are also dangerous places to be, as they are easily swept away by a rain-swollen tide, only to re-appear in a different shape somewhere else.

In places where the estuaries have been filling with mud since the last Ice Age, the mud deposits may be as much as 100 feet deep, cunningly concealed by a shimmering, iridescence surface layer. Here the mud – (Elemental Earth) is in contact with life-giving sunlight (Elemental Fire), (Elemental) water and (Elemental) air – that support the chain of life from algae and bacteria, through worms and shellfish, to flora and fauna. A truly magical environment.

- Without risk, collect a small glass jar of mud from the mudflat and, if you live away from the shore, this – along with your jars of sand and seawater – will be necessary ingredients for magical working.

- Make sure that there are no sea-creatures lurking in the mud, or they will die if removed from their natural environment.

Much of this sea-land around the world is being reclaimed for development, and as about half the world's population lives on, or within 60 miles of a coast, so we must learn to make the best use of this powerful, magical generator while it's still accessible.

Tidal waves and races
Local currents are movements of water that are the result of localised interaction between tidal forces and the shapes of the coastlines, such as the flow into and out of bays, for example. It is this movement of water that brings about local or tidal currents, and they can be especially dangerous where large volumes of water are funnelled through narrow channels around promon-

tories, between islands and up estuaries. At particular locations, they can cause phenomena such as tidal bores and whirlpools.

One of the most powerful, natural phenomena that can be harnessed magically is what is known as an *eagre* or *bore* – one of the most famous being the Severn Bore in England. Here, a tapering river mouth can convert the rising tide into a tidal wave: crowded together by the converging banks, the surging water becomes a powerful wave which rises, overhangs and collapses into a roaring wall of surf.

The Severn Bore travels upstream as a sequence of three or four unbroken waves and it is a fascinating sight to see the river suddenly reversed as the incoming tidal wave overcomes the natural flow of the water and flows upstream. In the River Severn it may reach up to 9¼ ft in 40 minutes, travelling at a speed of up to 13 mph! Though dangerous, it is easy to avoid, for the time of its arrival can be predicted, and unless conditions are favourable the tidal wave may completely fail to develop.

Most bores are unspectacular, but each year there are about 130 days with high and medium bores up to six feet in height, twice each day. The highest tides follow a few days after new and full moons, with the largest bores occurring during February to April and August to October, around the Spring and Autumn Equinoxes in the northern hemisphere. Check with local river folk to see if a similar phenomenon occurs nearby.

Any tide sweeping up a long narrow sea channel is especially powerful and *very* dangerous. In places where two tides meet, as off the north coast of Scotland, there are dangerous tidal races, a swift rush of the water, also known as rip-tides. There are places, too, where the tide forms whirlpools like the spectacular Naruto Whirlpool that occurs several times a day in the narrow channel linking the Sea of Japan to the Pacific Ocean. For these reasons, an inexperienced person should *never* venture out onto the water or sands alone.

- When attempting to 'power' a sea-witch's charm, visualise the swirling, surging waters of a bore, whirlpool or rip-tide to coincide with the actual event.

- **Do not, under any circumstances, attempt to go out into these waters for magical working. It is not necessary.**

Remember, from a magical perspective, when we refer to 'natural tides' we are also talking about the sea-tides (Elemental Water); earth-tides (Elemental Earth) and atmospheric-tides (Elemental Air) – all of which are created by cosmic-tides (Elemental Fire).

Think about it ...

The thin margin of shoreline, situated as it is between sea, sky and land is the point where we can truly plug-in to the swirling cosmic energies that gave birth to the Universe. So here, right on the edge of the seashore, we have a naturally created 'compass' or Circle in which to work, and access to the very energies that control Nature herself, all channelling into *our* sacred space! Is there any wonder that we cannot stress the point strongly enough that the sea is dangerous place to be?

Summoning up your witch power

A simple way of discovering when your own witch-power is in harmony with the natural tides is by using a simple, practical exercise to utilise the energies at a very basic level. The use of what we call witch-power is the transforming of our own personal energy into a tangible form; it is a way of proving to *ourselves* that the energy really *does* exist, and that we can have some degree of control over it. This 'energy' is the stuff of magic itself, which can be utilised in its raw state for certain magical operations.

Choose a quiet moment away from any distractions. Hold your hands in front of you at shoulder level, with the palms facing each other some six inches apart. Slowly move the palms together and at some point you will feel a sensation, i.e. a warm or cool breeze, tingling, etc. You may experience a slight resistance between your palms as if they are trying to push apart, or it may feel as if they are pulling together. Be assured that there are no pre-prescribed reactions for manifesting psychic ability and no two people will experience an identical result.

Try the exercise at different times in conjunction with the ebb and flow of the tide.

- Is the sensation stronger, or different, at high tide than at low tide?

- Is there any change in sensation between the two daily tides?

Over a period of time, you will build up a pattern of high and low energy yields, closely interacting with all the natural tides. Try the exercise at different times of the month and record the results:

Sea-tides (Elemental Water): At the time of local high and low tides.

Earth-tides (Elemental Earth): At the time of the full and new moon

Atmospheric-tides (Elemental Air): At the time of the moon's first and third quarter.

Cosmic-tides (Elemental Fire): At a time of increased sunspot activity.

You may find that each one produces its own distinct sensation, or that some produce no sensation at all. Ultimately, you will discover your own unique time for magical working ... but this will not be the same for you as it is for me, or for other readers of this book.

Weather lore

As Paul Goldsack so rightly points out in *Weatherwise*, a seaman's ability to 'read the sky' should not be dismissed as quaint folk-lore. The lore about clouds and sky colour has been bequeathed to us by past generations of seamen and country folk and are among the most valuable of all weather signs, if only we know how to read them. 'They are more reliable than most of the bewitching adages about birds and beasts; just as knowing as messages in the wind, and just as apparent as the ups and downs of a barometer – once we learn to see again.'

Our weather conditions do not depend so much on the direction from which the wind is blowing, as from its original 'source', which may be hundreds of miles away. In studying the behaviour of the winds, we are constantly reminded that this planet is continually spinning from west to east, pulling the atmosphere with it. What we also know, is that all times and depths of the sea tides are greatly affected by prevailing winds. For example, winds from the north-west to north-east increase these depths, and may cause high water to occur earlier than the tidal predictions on east coasts. Winds from the south-east through south to south-west, may cause tides to fall short of the predictions, and high water may occur later than expected.

One of the most reliable signs of all, however, is the colour of the sky, which provides the first indications on the day's weather, the most well-known being:

Red sky at night, sailor's delight;
Red sky in the morning, sailor's warning.

From the scientific viewpoint this also makes sense, because the soft pink under-belly of cloud, coloured by the sunset, indicates clear sky and dry air to the west. As most of our British weather comes in from the west, it shows that for a period of time, fine weather will follow. A 'red' sky can range from a warm pink to a day-glo red and those who have time to study the data about such things, tell us that this old saying qualifies for a 'reliability factor' close on 100%.

On the opposite side of the coin, we usually think of a blue sky as being associated with fine weather, but this is not always the case. It all depends on the *shade* of blue. For example: a very dark blue sky against which the clouds are sharply defined is a forerunner of stormy weather, but a soft, light blue means settled weather. And we all know that the bright coppery-coloured tints around cloud edges are a sign of electric disturbance in the atmosphere, which brings thunder-storms.

Puffy clouds, heavily tinted violet, usually bring on a spell of easterly winds, although this generally occurs during the winter months when the days are cold and cloudy, but with no rainfall. Grey skies usually mean rain, particularly when a blue sky gradually changes to a grey, ashen colour that spreads as far as the eye can see. The latter should not be confused with the murky, yellowish-grey gloom that approaches from the east during periods of drought, and often mistaken for a gathering storm. In fact, yellow is one of the worst colours, especially at sunset, and is most feared by sailors. It is the colour that warns of approaching storms, heavy gales and rain.

Send in the clouds

There are ten basic types of cloud world-wide, which are classified by their appearance and the sea-witch should begin by learning to recognise the following formations:

Cirrus (high level): The most common type of high-level cloud that is thin and wispy and often known as 'mare's tails'. Their appearance usually means that the ground-level wind will soon strengthen.

Cirrocumulus (high level): The clouds consist entirely of ice crystals that appear as white patches or spherical masses. These are arranged in regular patterns, often resembling ripples on a sandy beach or, less frequently, straight lines. Air movement can also produce small, regularly arranged globular masses of cloud reminiscent of the markings on a mackerel (see **altocumulus**), hence the name 'mackerel sky'.

Cirrostratus (high level): The sun shining on these high-level clouds at dawn and dusk produces spectacular sunrises and sunsets. At other times of the day they appear as a white veil that makes the sky look milky ... not enough to obscure the sun or moon but it can produce a halo around them. Its appearance is usually a sign of approaching rain.

Altostratus (middle level): A layer of this cloud can be up to 10,000 feet thick and cover a very large area, appearing as a uniform, grey or slightly blue sheet of cloud. The sun and moon may be faintly visible through it, but more often the cloud is thick enough to obscure them completely. Its appearance usually heralds rain or snow.

Altocumulus (middle level): Associated with cold fronts and often form at night when the temperature is lower. Often seen to form rolls, arranged in lines or waves, or distinctive rounded masses as well as a 'mackerel' sky.

Nimbostratus (low level): Low grey cloud that is dark and shapeless, with a ragged base that blankets the sky and gives continuous rain. In sharp contrast, beneath the ragged base there is usually a glimpse of lighter sky. It may produce steady, persistent rain or snow.

Cumulus (low level): The clouds are fleecy and separate from each other with blue sky in between. This allows the sun to shine directly on the clouds, so they appear very white with clearly defined edges.

Stratus (low level): More common near mountains and coasts and if at ground level then stratus occurs as fog. Fog clears by the evaporation of its lowest layer, and any remaining fog becomes stratus cloud. The cloud often forms overnight in fine weather, especially over water.

Cumulonimbus (low level): These clouds produce thunderstorms, hailstorms and tornados, as well as torrential snow or rain. It is typically deep and large, with a dark menacing appearance and during a storm may be illuminated from within by lightning sparking.

Stratocumulus (low level): Rolls or rounded masses of darker cloud give a textured appearance. At dawn and dusk, the sunlight shining through any gaps may illuminate dust particles creating converging rays of light.

So ... rather than destroying magic within Nature, scientific explanations often *strengthen* magical belief. After all, a lot of what has passed for 'magic' in the past has its roots in ancient wisdom, and we should honour the fact that many of our ancestors' 'primitive' beliefs have since been exonerated by proven scientific fact. Don't forget it was Aleister Crowley who wrote that magick was a blend of science and art! Nevertheless, with so many commercial books on 'pagan spell culture', we are again in danger of becoming bogged down under a mantle of *contemporary* superstition, urban myth and fake-lore. By accepting science as part of our understanding, we widen our own grasp of the universal power that lies behind the quest for all true magical knowledge.

The seashore also offers opportunities for observing

'portents' or 'sights in the heavens' that are not always visible from inland. These phenomena, of course, demand a clear sky, and are best seen on moonless nights, although on the western shores it is possible to witness some of the most fantastic Turnereque seascapes imaginable, at any time of the day. Although they are all *natural phenomena*, there is nevertheless a magical quality about witnessing such happenings, and a sense of being in the right place at the right time; to being privy to something special. The opportunity should never be missed 'to stand and stare' – even at a reflected chain of coloured lights from the esplanade, in the night-time waters of the bay.

Towards nightfall a vague darkness may sometimes be seen rising slowly in the east – this is the *shadow of the earth*, cast by the setting sun upon the atmosphere.

Sea-sparkle, in autumn or late summer, is visible in breaking waves or wavelets, in water disturbed by oars, or the passage of nets, producing a waving wall of luminescence. The agitated water causes the light-chemical in luminous protozoan to combine with oxygen, which causes the sparkle, or 'burning of the waves'. In his *Survey of Cornwall* (1602) Richard Carew wrote of the phenomena: *'If the sea-water bee flashed with a sticke or oare, the same casteth a bright shining colour, and the drops thereof resemble sparckles of fire, as if the waves were turned into flames.'*

At the last gleam of sunset the famous 'green ray' may flash upwards from the skyline. Whoever catches a glimpse of the 'living light' will, so tradition runs, be magically blessed. Many occultists associate this with the Evening Star, or Venus since this is often the only 'star' visible at this special moment between sunset and dusk.

An eerie brightness above the western horizon where the sun has set, is the afterglow and its counterpart, visible in the east a little before sunrise, is the false dawn – the two forming the zodiacal light. During the night a faintly gleaming circle may cross the sky from east to west, it is the counter-glow, moving so as to keep opposite the sun.

Moon-glade refers to the 'path' of moonlight across the sea, broken and catching the motion of the waves, between the moon and the watcher. In Tudor times, the term 'moonshine in the water' was a common phrase for empty notions or dreams.

From northerly regions, the Aurora Borealis, or Northern Lights may be seen flickering in the night sky. This occurs most often in the spring and autumn, especially at times of increased sunspot activity.

On dark nights the surface of the sea may become luminous. The combined phosphorescence of countless microscopic creatures in the water produces this effect. Though not so brilliant as that of the glow-worm, their united gleam can be surprisingly bright.

Atmospheric conditions may give distant objects the eerie appearance of being nearer than they are. This occasionally produces a *mirage*, a reflection above the horizon of ships, or a distant shore hidden below it. Distortion usually makes the reflections unrecognisable, often giving the impression of fairy-castles and unearthly landscapes.

St Elmo's Fire is a gleam of electrical origin occasionally visible on the tips of masts and spars. Though it appears in thundery weather, it does not flash like lightning, being a harmless form of static electricity.

The highest clouds, known as noctilucent clouds, shine after dark on clear nights. They are found at heights about 50 miles above the earth and consist of ice-coated dust particles from outer space.

Haloes can be seen round the sun and moon on about one day in three, but are only really noticeable round the moon. On clear nights the moon may have a white luminous ring; if it is cloudy the halo is tinged with the colours of the rainbow. Haloes are caused by refraction of light through ice crystals, and often precede a storm.

Now we have been introduced to the magical world of the seashore, we can begin to build up the knowledge that will help us perfect the powers of a sea-witch.

Spring tide ritual

Using all this information about witch-power, tides and weather, it is possible for the sea-witch to calculate the *precise* moment when all the Elemental attributes are synchronised at the shore-line, in order to draw the maximum energy to power a magical working. This is why it is much more important to consult *local* tide charts than to work out traditional planetary correspondences from a 17th century *grimoire*, or a contemporary spell-book.

Use the following two-line extract from the poem, *Sea-Fever*, by John Masefield as a chant, repeating the lines over and over to raise the concentration of power:

'I must go down to the seas again, for the call of the running tide
Is a wild call and a clear call that may not be denied;'

If possible, stand at the very water's edge and gaze out to sea, imagining the power of the sea surging forward from a point way out on the horizon. The beauty of being able to stand and stare at the sea at any time of day or night, is that ordinary, everyday folk will be doing the same, and so the sea-witch does not look out of place, either on the beach, esplanade or the cliff top.

Repeat the chant over and over, and feel the power from the Deep building up and rolling towards you. You don't need to bellow at the top of your voice, repeating the words over and over in your head will produce the same effect. Fix your sight on a wave as far out to sea as possible, and draw it towards where you stand on the beach or break-water. As the waves break against the shore, collect a small jar of seawater for future magical use, because even the smallest wave is part of the whole, vast ocean.

As you become more familiar with the powerful energies generated at the seashore, the more ambitious your magical workings will become, but be mindful of one final word of warning. NEVER underestimate the dangers of the sea, and time spent in the company of locals who understand the natural dangers, may just save your life. Even highly experienced sailors never take the sea for granted.

Magical tasks and exercises

- Add to your magical library several natural history books concerning the seashore and weather lore and, if you are near to the coast, make sure you have an up-to-date listing of the local tides. For those living inland, the daily broadsheet newspapers or the internet will supply general information about the daily tides. Or contact the harbour master on any of the great tidal rivers.

- Familiarise yourself with this new way of thinking about magical tides, and record the readings of your own witch-power exercises in a personal Magical Diary. Keep experimenting at different times and under different conditions until the process becomes automatic.

- Instead of synchronising your magical workings according to any popular 'wheel of the year', try working with the natural tides that are having their effect on the earth and its atmosphere on a *day-to-day* basis.

- Take some time to watch the sky, even if it is through a windowpane, and try to become more aware of the changing clouds and colour patterns, and learn to understand what they are telling you.

- A sea-witch works during the day as well as after dark, so if your trips to the beach are restricted to daylight hours, this will not cause any problems with your magical development.

Chapter Two

Four Sea Interludes

Despite the fact that we live in an age of computer technology, many traditional fishermen and sea-farers still use magic and ritual to protect themselves to this day. It may be true to say that fishing communities have been the most superstitious of all – and especially the fishermen themselves. Even those who belonged to a church when they were ashore, still feared and respected the old pagan gods while at sea. The reason for these customs lasting well into the 20th century was no doubt due to the dangers the men faced when they were at the mercy of the elements day after day.

In *The Penguin Guide to Superstitions*, author Steve Roud offers the explanation that such shared traditions thrived best where there was a strong, tightly knit community, which was inwardly rather than outwardly focussed. In this environment there was a strong sense that superstitions provided 'rules' covering the trivia of everyday life, and functioned as a sign as to who was in, and who was outside the group. 'Men from fishing families will know the rules, outsiders will not. Youngsters will thus be particularly keen to learn, in order to prove themselves fit for membership.'

So strong were the pagan elements surrounding the sea, that in some fishing communities, clergymen and the church were forbidden topics up to comparatively recent times, showing that the respect for the older elements were still respected more than any fear of, or support for, the church. In fact, the mere sight of 'the gentleman in black' as a fisherman made his way down to the harbour, was enough to make him cancel the trip if he was really superstitious.

Another ancient custom, thought to be another survival of pagan sea-god worship, was observed well into the 20th century at the old fishing village of Abbotsbury, in England. On 13th May, the fishermen's families constructed large garlands of flowers on wooden frames – one for each fishing boat. The garlands were carried round the houses and then blessed before being taken out to sea and thrown overboard. The procession took place up to the present day, but the flowers were placed on the war memorial as a tribute to the dead.

In more recent years, the number of pleasure-craft now moored in coastal harbours by far outweighs those of commercial sailors, but there is a noticeable absence of traditional amulets on even the largest of modern boats. Perhaps it's because few 'fair-weather' sailors venture far from land that they don't feel the need to protect their boat and themselves from the unexpected mood-swings of the sea. To be on the safe side, however, it may be provident for *anyone* setting sail, to offer some small tribute to the ocean gods before leaving the safety of the harbour walls. In the Mediterranean, for example, an eye is painted on the prow of a boat to ward off ill-luck, dating back to ancient times.

According to *Folk-lore, Myth & Legend in Britain*, the destiny of a ship was once thought to be so closely bound up with that of her carved figurehead that one could not sink without the other. To sail in a ship without a figurehead was highly dangerous, for the figurehead embodied the ship's soul and the vessel's painted name was part of her identity, which had been chosen with great care. It would have also been unthinkable to set sail without some form of obeisance, and many setting sail for the New World would have taken many of these superstitions with them.

'The prevalence of figureheads carved to resemble naked women probably resulted from the pre-Christian practice of dedicating ships to goddesses'… and may explain why ships are always regarded as feminine. There may also be a link with the belief recorded by Pliny almost 2000 years ago that 'a storm may

24

be lulled by a woman uncovering her body out to sea'. Conversely, some sailors still believe that it is unlucky to go to sea with a woman aboard, or even to meet a woman on the walk down to the harbour prior to setting sail.

As an island people, much of our history (and that of those ancestors who sailed away), is bound up with the sea since it has provided a protective barrier against invasion throughout the ages. At the same time, even from ancient times, it has brought the world to our shores for a commercial exchange of goods … so it is not surprising that the old customs involve a considerable amount of propitiatory rites to protect both the people and the craft that braved the unpredictable tides and currents of the ocean.

With this in mind, Barry Cunliffe, Professor of European Archaeology at Oxford, and author of *Facing The Ocean*, observes:

Those who face the ocean will always be in awe of the uncontrollable power of the waves and the swells, and the inexorable, reassuring, strength of the sea's rhythm. However informed we may be of the nature of the sea in terms of modern science, it is difficult not to recall in some half-remembered way, deeply rooted ancestral beliefs in the personality of the ocean.

Apart from occasional landslips, the destruction of our coastlines is so gradual that it often goes unrecorded. Nevertheless, the eastern coast of North America itself has changed a lot in the past 15,000 years with sea level rising to drown many ancient valleys. And as ancient maps and records do show, thousands of acres with many villages and several flourishing towns have vanished from the coastlines of Europe, together with the countryside around them. In England, East Anglia once extended into the North Sea and without the artificial protection of sea-walls, the destruction would be greater still. There is also the loss of upwards of 30 Humberside villages along a two and a half mile strip of land between the headlands, which have vanished since Roman times.

These lost landscapes have given rise to many legends. Off the English south coast, the Goodwin Sands were said to be the island of Lomea, which belonged to Godwine, Earl of the West Saxons. The island was drowned in a great storm of 1099 because, as legend tells us, an abbot of Canterbury used materials and money intended for sea-defences, to build the steeple of Tenterden church.

There is also evidence that other parts of the coast have sunk into the sea, since the river mouths of Devon and Cornwall are very different from the usual estuary. 'Long narrow inlets whose steep banks are clothed down to high tide level with vegetation, have a striking resemblance to inland valleys artificially damned to form reservoirs.'

Such drowned valleys – a Welsh example is Milford Haven in Pembrokeshire – also exist elsewhere in England, on the western coasts of Scotland and Ireland, and the eastern USA, such as Chesapeake Bay.

Off the British coast are a number of submerged forests (usually pine) that flourished some 8000 years ago, when the sea level was lower, and many of the remains belong to species that normally grow some distance inland. At East Sussex, the present sea-level is 20-30 feet higher than when the trees were growing, and beneath the Dogger Bank in the English Channel and elsewhere, are submerged peat-bogs and beds of leaf-mould. St Michael's Mount, near Penzance, for example, has a Cornish name, which means 'the ancient rock in the midst of the woods' – it is now an island connected with the shore only at low tide.

Many fossilised remains also show evidence of more than one change of sea level. Petrified forests, where the tree roots and trunks have been transformed into stone, such as those found on the cliff edge near Lulworth Cove, in England, indicate that the trees which grew on dry land, had to sink beneath the sea to become 'petrified' and to rise above the waves again to emerge as fossils. Some rocks teem with fossils: there are limestones consisting largely of fossil seaweeds, corals or shell-fish and only drastic coastal changes could have raised them above the sea. Another example are the cliff formations in the Bay of Fundy, Canada that are former beaches raised by glacial rebound.

- This would be the perfect setting to perform any magical working connected with Time and Otherworld.

These 'strangenesses' usually appear after the winter storms, when sand from the beach has been carried out below the low-water mark. Those who only visit the coast in the summer are unaware of these seasonal changes, and would not recognise a familiar sandy beach in its winter form with rock and shingle exposed.

Perhaps the most famous of these ancient British seashore discoveries, however, is possibly Seahenge, the timber circle found in 1998 on the exposed beach at Holme-next-the Sea. This small circle of 55 timber posts, surrounded the lower trunk and roots of a large oak tree, weighing about 2.5 tonnes, which had been lowered into the pit upside-down, so that the roots were above ground. Similar rituals were carried out by the indigenous people of Lapland and north Norway, whereby their world and Otherworld were obviously connected by an ancient form of 'as above, so below'.

Most witches will be familiar with Yssdrasil, from Scandinavian mythology; the world ash tree that stands at the centre of the Universe, connecting the heavens, the earth and the underworld. Seahenge may show that some similar belief existed in Neolithic and Bronze Age Britain long before the Norse invasion, but the more interesting factor is that constructed just before 2000BCE, in the Early Bronze Age, the ceremonies and rituals enacted there, *close to the shores of the North Sea* were,

27

according to archaeologist Francis Pryor in *Britain BC*, already very ancient, 'with roots in Britain that were then even older than Christianity is today'.

Another lost landscape can be found in Welsh tradition, where Cartref-y-Gwaelod, described as 'that most beautiful fertile and pleasant vale', is now submerged beneath the waters of Cardigan Bay. According to legend, the sea was kept at bay by a system of dykes and sluices and, either by negligence or malice during a night of revelry, the sluice gates were opened and the land flooded, with only a handful of the inhabitants making it to safety.

There are other similar Welsh folk-tales, such as the disappearance of Llys Helig beneath Lake Bala; and the destruction of the kingdom of Tyno Helig, which spread across the area now known as Colwyn Bay. Legend says that the latter's flooding was due to divine wrath being visited on the last king. It was a long-held belief that when the tide was low the ruins of the sunken palace were visible from fishing boats: an underwater survey revealed that these were in fact a five-acre expanse of natural rock formations!

Because of its Arthurian connections, the mythical land of Lyonesse is possibly the most famous of the 'lost land' legends. It was said to stretch away from the coast of Cornwall, and included a mighty forest where King Arthur and his knights and ladies used to hunt. It became the 'Lost Land of Lyonesse' with only a few of its hills remaining above the Atlantic: now the Scilly Isles. Only Trevilian escaped on a horse fast enough to outrun the incoming waves.

Although all the 'lost land' legends demonstrate a remarkably similarity, it is doubtful whether these landmasses actually disappeared at a time that can be pinpointed with any historical accuracy. Barry Cunliffe in *Facing The Ocean*, offers the possible explanation that lying behind the traditions is an actual event that passed into folk memory, and later spread along the Atlantic seaways during the period of increased mobility in the 5‾6th centuries. Perhaps, he suggests, these stories, reflected in folk-lore, offer an explanation for the unstable equilibrium between land and sea. Land is reclaimed from the sea by men and later taken back by the tidal powers of the ocean – 'the sea gives, the sea takes, and all the time the sea demands the lives of men mediated by the longings of the powerful presiding female spirit.'

There are also numerous superstitions about sea-witches, who had power over the winds and who have long been feared along Britain's coastline. When a Shetland witch wanted to wreck a ship, she stood on her head and chanted: *'Sweery, sweery, linkum-loo! Do to them as I now do.'* Sir Francis Drake was said to have enlisted the help of witches to raise the storms that defeated the Spanish Armada ... Napoleon was thwarted by witches when he was poised to invade England ... in exactly the same way as those witches who raised the power on Lammas Eve in 1940, to stop Operation Sealion, Hitler's invasion at the start of WWII – several dying as a result.

Details of this last extraordinary rite were recorded by both Jack Bracelin in *Gerald Gardner: Witch* and by Patricia Crowther in *Lid Off the Cauldron*. The story is now part of British Craft lore, and tells of how a group of witches met at night in the New Forest where the Great Circle was cast; the great Cone of Power raised and directed in the general direction of Hitler. The command was given: *'You cannot cross the Sea. You cannot cross the Sea. You cannot come: you cannot come!'* As Patricia Crowther says in her book: 'Whether you believe in the efficacy of this ritual or not, the facts are that the invasion plans were put off, and Hitler turned his attentions to Russia.'

Despite their fairy-tale malevolence, witches have always been a recognised part of the community and often turned to in times of need. There is a Shetland story of the islanders who suffered serious and ongoing depredations at the hands of a ship's crew who regularly moored off the island. In desperation the community leaders turned to the local wise woman for help.

Having heard their tale she replied that '*I canna du ony good, an I canna du muckle herm; bit ye gang an tell da folk ta mak fast dir boats and tak weelo about dir grains o corn,*' The men departed and secured their boats, stacks of corn and all loose property. That night a wild storm burst on the Atlantic and in the morning they saw the ship had foundered on the rocks. *[The Penguin Guide to Superstitions of Britain & Ireland]*

High winds and storms at sea were often attributed to the malevolent actions of witches, but the clergy who were attempting to inflict their beliefs on the populace were the ones who generally recorded the stories. An early example is given by Bede in the *History of the English Church and People* (c731CE), of when Bishops Germanus and Lupus were sailing to Britain 'to save the faithful from the Pelagian heresy' in 429CE:

They had safely sailed half-way on their voyage from Gaul with a favourable wind when they were suddenly subjected to the hostile powers of devils who were furious that such men should dare to recall the Britons to the way of salvation. The sails were torn to shreds by the gale, the skill of the sailors was defeated, and the safety of the ship depended on prayer rather than on seamanship.

Running true to form, the bishops would have exploited their 'miraculous' survival as a demonstration of the power of the Christian god over the demonic forces of the Old Ones. A witch's ability to raise storms was one of the charges recorded in the infamous *Malleus Maleficarum* and the Church of Rome made it official:

That devils and their disciples can by witchcraft cause lightnings and hailstorms and tempests ... Therefore it is reasonable to conclude that, just as easily as they raise hailstorms, so can they cause lightning and storms at sea; and so no doubt at all remains on these points.

Beneficent witches, on the other hand, were often called upon to provide a weather spell in the form of a knotted string. The following was recorded c1350 in the *Polychronicon* by Ranulph Higden:

'[In the Isle of Man] *witchcraft is exercised much, for women there be wont to sell wind to the shipmen coming to that country, as included under three knots of thread, so that they will unloose the knots like as they will have the wind to blow.*'

In addition to calling upon the services of the local witch or wise-woman, many of the smaller fishing communities revered their own local spirit or guardian. For example, local folk-lore tells of the 'Whooper' of Sennen Cove, which appears to have been a form of *genius loci* from Cornwall. The Whooper made 'whooping' sounds from within a thick blanket of mist that sometimes formed in perfectly clear weather over the cove. Apart from foretelling severe storms, the Whooper's protective qualities had the uncanny ability to prevent any fishermen from passing through to the open sea whenever a storm threatened. One day, ignoring the warning, two men decided to battle their way through the mist and they were never seen or heard of again ... but neither was the Whooper, who left the cove and took away the community's protection.

There is probably a perfectly natural explanation for the Whooper, and all the other strange noises that can be heard along the cliff pathways. Waves rushing into a tapering cavern that opens inland can emerge as a violent and noisy jet of water, air and spray, producing a blow-hole. Spurting from a blow-hole at the end of a lengthy cavern, it may seem to burst mysteriously out of the ground. Similarly, a blow-hole emerging at the summit of a cliff many not necessarily emit spray but instead a gust of air, strong enough to be perceptible and to disturb the grass, together with audible sound effects. A simple landslide or rock fall would be enough to stop the phenomena.

The sea-witch has impressive antecedents in British folk-lore but again, the main feature of working within this environment is a complete understanding of the elements, tides and weather. The sea-witch can also use the water-margin for lucid dreaming and pathworking, for it is here, where the water meets the land, that we can truly experience the magic of the seashore.

But first we need to find a special amulet that has come from the Deep ...

Spell to bring a pebble amulet

The text of the following invocation refers to the fact that a large number of the pebbles on our beaches have been washed down from 'high mountains', being tumbled and smoothed in the process. It is a journey that may have taken many hundreds, if not thousands of years, as each small piece of rock tumbles down through mountain streams and into the riverbeds, only to be swept along in the flood to be deposited as shingle on the beach at the estuary. The most common shingle feature is the 'fringe' of pebbles familiar to holidaymakers, which is formed when the action of the waves deposits a bank of pebbles at the water margin.

The best places to look

Though shingle is present on most beaches, it is often shifting and unstable. The exceptions are the mud flats of expansive estuaries; on sandy beaches; and where the sea does not recede from the cliffs. There are, however, some world famous shingle beds that are especially noteworthy and provide exceptionally good samples. The foremost British example is Chesil Beach on the Dorset coast, once described as the 'most extensive and most extraordinary accumulation of shingle in the world'. While shingle beaches are most commonly associated with Western Europe, examples are found in Bahrain, the United States, and in a number of other world regions such as the east coast of New Zealand's South Island.

What you are likely to find

Generally speaking pebbles fall into three distinct shapes: spheres, which are almost round, for a perfectly round pebble (like a marble) would be a very rare find indeed; ovoids, which are egg-shaped; and flattened ovoids that come from thin plates or layers of rock, such as slate. Unless you have some prior geological knowledge, it is doubtful at first whether you will be able to recognise the parent rock from which your pebble originally came.

Invocation to Neptune

Of Neptune's empire let us sing,
At whose command the waves obey;
To whom the rivers tribute pay,
Down the high mountain sliding;
To who the scaly nation yields
Homage for the crystal fields
Wherein they dwell:
And every sea-god pays a gem
Yearly out of his wat'ry call
To deck great Neptune's diadem.

This extract from Thomas Campion's *A Hymn in Praise of Neptune* (1567–1620) probably recalls the occasion of the Roman Emperor Caligula's military campaign against Neptune, when the spoils of this engagement were chests full of pebbles and seashells. Unlike Caligula, we cannot be fooled into thinking that our beaches will yield any precious stones, although there are several of the semi-precious varieties to be found.

Only on a *very* rare occasion will your amulet fall into this category, because there among the shingle *are* tiny pieces of jet and amber – not to mention amethyst, rose quartz, citrine, cairngorm, chalcedony, agate, onyx, jasper and carnelian. Amber is fossilised resin from pine trees that lived about 50 million years ago and preserved in Ice Age glaciers. When they melted, it was deposited in the seas of Europe – chiefly the Baltic – and is often washed up on the north-eastern beaches of Britain. Some pieces have insects trapped inside the sticky resin as it oozed out of the trees. Amber found on British beaches is rarely larger than a small pebble, though a piece was found in Suffolk in the 19th century weighing 13lbs, and fetched the princely sum of £4000! In reality, your amulet will probably be a smoothed pebble of granite, flint, sandstone or limestone ...

Having intoned your 'Invocation to Neptune', walk along the high water mark, where the pebbles have been thrown by the waves, and think about ... nothing. Rake around with your hands among the pebbles to see what lies lower down. More likely than not, the single pebble that catches your eye will have little value as far as anyone else is concerned. When you have made your selection, take the pebble to the water's edge and wash it in the sea. This is the only cleansing you will need to do as the whole tumbling, smoothing, immersion process has been a natural one, and to 'ritually' cleanse the pebble would destroy its natural properties. Remember to leave some form of offering in the form of food for the seagulls or other shore creatures, and place your amulet in a special pouch.

We should never lose sight of the fact that the myths of many cultures recognise the sea as an element of primal mystery and creation. From the ancient Egyptians and the Japanese, to the Koran and the Old Testament, this primordial water represents the chaotic 'nothingness' out of which life was formed. Rebecca Rupp in *Four Elements*, also writes of the character the ancients gave to their sea-gods, in that all shared similar temperaments: 'moody, hot-tempered and mean'. Storm-wrecked Viking ships were said to plummet into the jaws of Aegir; victims of more recent centuries, sank into Davy Jones's locker.

The sea has always been man's 'unsolved mystery' but everywhere in the world it is celebrated in paint, poetry, prose and music. [The chapter headings in this book refer to classical music pieces taking their theme from the sea: *Sea Fever* (Ireland); *Four Sea Interludes* (Britten); *Sea Drift* (Delius); *Sea and Sky* (Finnissy); *Sea Pictures* (Elgar); *The Roaring of a Wave* (Sibelius); *Toward the Sea* (Takemitsu) and *Calm Sea* (Mendelssohn).] It features in religion and folk-lore and, as well as having magical powers itself, was believed to be populated by all manner of the divine, semi-divine and demons, with Nereids and Oceanides (nymphs of the sea), apparently being the only creatures to look kindly upon humans! Artists, such as Carl von Marr in his vision of *Sea Nymphs,* were still depicting this romantic imagery, well into the 19th century.

The ocean's place in the collective unconscious is a channel of immense power ... and this is the power with which we wish to connect during our quest.

You will probably not be able to explain why, out of all the pebbles on the beach, this particular one appeared to answer your call. What you must keep in mind is that this tiny pebble was 'born' when the Earth itself was young, and will be far more magically potent than any expensive piece of mined and polished crystal from a New Age shop.

The power of the stones

• Naturally white stones are rare and prized for their luck-bringing, or curative powers, by using the following chant:

Lucky white stone, lucky white stone
Bring me luck when I go home.

- An old Irish belief says to place a white stone in dark bowl of clear water if you wish to discover who is causing mischief, and wait for the images to appear in your mind.

- Stones with a natural hole in them, i.e. hagstones, are to be found on the beach. They are considered to be extremely lucky and protective, especially if they are given or received as a gift. They can be hung in a building to protect home and livestock, carried about the person to avert all negative influences, or hung on the bedstead to prevent nightmares.

- A holed stone was valued for its intrinsic power, and there is no evidence that it needed any special treatment or preparation before use, although some believe that it will only begin to work once it has been threaded on a piece of cord.

- Rare pieces of chalcedony can be found on the Scottish coast, and on the eastern and southern coats of England, of which an old rhyme tells us:

Pierced and worn upon the neck or hand
A sure success in lawsuits 'twill command

Magical tasks and exercises

- Begin to make a study of marine and fishermen's superstitions, and keep a note of them in separate categories in your Magical Journal. This will help you understand how the sea-witch looks at the creatures and objects that make up his or her 'personal universe'.

- Start to observe the behaviour of the seagulls and learn about the lore surrounding them. In coastal areas, the birds were viewed with suspicion, or at least caution, but the reasons varied. The most common belief is that their cries are those of drowned seamen and therefore to kill one is considered extremely unlucky. For the sea-witch, the cry of the gulls would be a constant companion, whether on the beach, the cliffs or the harbour.

- Keep an eye open for a suitable piece of driftwood that can serve as a sea-witch's wand or staff. Being immersed in brine for a long time can either make the wood very tough or very brittle, so select the wood with care. Allow the piece to dry naturally rather than by artificial means and do not 'cleanse' as the wood will lose its natural magical properties.

- Driftwood can also produce the most amazing flames as the dried salt burns in colours of vivid blues and greens. A driftwood fire on the beach after dark is a truly magical experience.

Chapter Three

Sea Drift

The sea is not merely salty, it is *bitter*, consisting of brine, a strong solution of material washed down from the land. Sodium chloride (or common salt) predominates, but many other chemicals are also present, with traces at least of all the elements. Which is why, of course, the consecrated water used in traditional magical rites is basic brine. Another point to consider is that all living creatures – including humans – are descended from creatures of the sea: human blood does indeed have certain affinities with brine!

Should we need to artificially create this consecrated water, 'Maldon salt', obtained from any good quality delicatessen or supermarket, makes the best solution. Maldon salt is *world* renowned for its quality and tradition, and comes in the form of light, feathery crystals produced from the tidal waters of the River Blackwater in England. Look carefully at a 'pinch' in the palm of your hand and reflect on the minute, hollow pyramid crystals, which reproduce the simple molecular structure of natural sodium chloride.

The ancient community of Maldon (actually some 10 miles inland) has harvested the salt since Roman times; a thousand years later, 45 productive saltpans on the Blackwater Estuary were listed in the Doomsday Book. Maldon is situated on one of the most saline rivers in Britain, its name deriving from the word 'brackish', rather than 'black', and is surrounded by acres of marshland that floods at high tide. Seawater is trapped in gullies and evaporates, especially on dry, windy days, and the following tide draws the brine from these pools. This effect is particularly pronounced during the spring tides that occur twice a month, and it is this natural 'harvest' that gives the Maldon Crystal Salt Company its raw product.

Salt is, of course, a *vital* ingredient in magical working. Not only does it provide the basic solution for consecrated water, it can also be representative of Elemental Earth, since halite or sodium chloride crystals, are one of the Earth's natural minerals. Salt represents one of the alchemical forms of energy that unites Mercury and Sulphur, and is represented by The Empress in the Tarot. It is also a 'binding' agent, in that it plays an important part in initiatory rites and, symbolically, if someone has shared 'bread and salt' they would be breaking the obligation of hospitality or chivalry to then cause you harm.

Salt also plays a protective role in a range of contexts. There is a widespread superstition that salt must never be borrowed, only given away, as to return it would only bring trouble. If you sprinkle salt on the floor after unwelcome visitors have left, they will not trouble you again; while a ring of salt around the house will keep negative forces at bay. Salt can be used in most protective rites, including those of banishing and witch-bottling. For all these reasons, a sea-witch should keep a small bottle of sea-water at home for emergency use.

Beachcombing

The average sandy beach is made up from tons of tiny particles of rock and shell, resulting from years of weathering and erosion by the sea. The sea breaks rocks from the cliffs and the waves lash them against the rocky foreshore, breaking them into even smaller pieces. Once the particles of rock and shell (from sea creatures that once clung to them), are tiny enough to float in the sea, they are carried along the coast by the waves. Since, as we have seen, the waves are created by winds far out to sea, the direction from which the waves approach the shore is determined by the direction of the prevailing winds. The natural ebb and flow of the waves, as well as that of the tides, carries the sand with them up the beach – until it is finally deposited at the water margin.

- Patterns in the sand created by the receding tide can be used for divination where slight depressions are caused by water gouging out some sand as it flows back to the sea. The sand is deposited a little further down the beach to form a variety of patterns.

- Empty shells on the beach may provide useful clues to the types of creature living beneath the surface … but clusters of empty shells can also be used as *in situ* divinatory tools.

- Ask your question and see what impressions you get from these natural phenomena.

In fact, the sea and shore can provide us with most of the equipment the sea-witch needs for magical working. On the beach, the high-water mark is evident by the line of material left behind by the retreating waves, and often a depository for pebbles forced inland from deeper waters by the winter storms. It is here that we are more than likely to find other items that could be used in our rituals, in addition to the pebble amulet previously acquired. How about this simple chant to help find something suitable?

Power of the Tides, Power of the Deep
Have you a gift for me to keep?

The pebbles of a shingle beach are almost devoid of water and, ground together by the waves, would soon crush and destroy any living things but here at the high-water mark there are all manner of treasures to be found that can be utilised as amulets and working tools:

- bleached and twisted pieces of driftwood
- a wide variety of shells
- tumbled pebbles and hagstones
- fossils uncovered by a cliff-fall
- coloured, polished glass
- large, smoothed altar stones
- marine egg-cases known as a 'mermaid's purse'
- and, for the less squeamish, the skull of a fish or sea-bird

The breakwater

Generally referring to a timber frame, or low broad wall (also called a *groyne*), built to control sea encroachment by checking wave action on the foreshore. Shingle is swept away from one side and piles up on the other, where it is moved up the beach at right angles to the waves. If the tides are too strong, there will be little growth of seaweed, but in more sheltered spots small rock pools will form in the lee of the breakwater.

- This is an ideal spot to look for amulets and working tools.

Driftwood

There are all kinds of pieces of wood washed up on the beach and all of it has its magical uses. Those sea-witches who have easy access to the beach will have their own store of wood pulled well away from the high-tide mark to dry out. Water-logged wood is extremely heavy to carry and it is better to leave it to dry out naturally before attempting to carry it home. As we know, long-term immersion in the sea can cause wood to become immensely tough, or extremely brittle, so unless you can recognise the tree from whence it came, you'll have to wait a while before discovering whether it is suitable for making into a magical tool ... or merely for use as firewood.

Although it's not advisable to light a fire on summer tourist beaches, there are stretches of coastline that lends itself to a discreet off-season bonfire now and again. You don't have to indulge in a full-scale ritual to enjoy the ambiance of a night-time beach-party. A couple of like-minded friends, a few bottles of wine, supper with plenty of hot coffee or soup, and the potency of the seashore can turn out to be a wholly magical affair. Don't be surprised to receive a visit from the local police ... that's why it's a good idea to take spare mugs: for those uninvited guests.

Finally, make sure that the fire is out before you leave. Smothering the embers with sand puts out the flames but it will trap in the heat, and a dog or child could still be badly burned if it ran across the remains while out for an early morning stroll.

Some most amazing shapes can be found among the piles of driftwood and if you prefer to work with a Wand, then a truly original design can be yours for the asking. A stout Staff is also a useful tool for poking around in the shingle and to test the depth of rock pools, but it also a traditional witch's trademark, more often referred to in traditional Craft as a 'stang'. These items are highly personal tools and should be created to serve your own instinct, rather than because of any instructions given in a book. The wood has come, quite literally, out of the sea and will already be highly charged with oceanic energy and needs no cleansing or consecrating.

This also applies to those amazing natural 'sculptures' of driftwood that can be used in the home or garden for ornament, or flower arrangement.

- If taking driftwood indoors, leave the wood under cover to dry out and keep brushing away the sand that will be hidden in every tiny crevice.

- A simple piece of driftwood in an alcove, set against (for example) a backdrop of a traditional Japanese sea scroll (or any sea picture), would prove a discreet sea-witch's altar without visitors being any the wiser.

Shells

The best time to collect shells is at low spring tide, which occurs for a few days every fortnight, coinciding with the full and new moon, and low tide – when the maximum amount of shore is uncovered – and will yield the largest collection.

One of the most common sights on the beach is a discarded scallop shell, which we can pass by without a second glance ... but this would be a mistake. The scallop has figured in the affairs of man from earliest times, permeating all cultures and all periods of history. This sea creature is a mollusc: a member of a very large group of animals that includes oysters, whelks, octopuses and sea-slugs.

It has existed in its recognised form for about 150 million years, with some geologists tracing its remains in rocks 300 million years old. The almost round outline, with ribs radiating like a Roman comb, caused Pliny to call them *pecten*. B. Woledge, Fielden Professor of French at University College, London commented that in appearance no other molluscan shells have so pleasing a design and range of colours as pectin shells, 'and it is small wonder that they have stimulated man's imagination all over the world since ancient times.'

This is no exaggeration: the art of the classical world is strewn with scallop shells. Botticelli bore Aphrodite from the Deep in one; Greek craftsmen used the image on earthenware vessels and burial urns; an ancestral altar in the courtyard of a Roman house at Herculaneum was decorated with one; during the Roman period the shell appeared on every type of monument, including tombs and coffins; while later architects incorporated the design into the porches of London houses.

There is no way of telling for certain whether there was any religious or symbolic purpose behind the image, but the repeated use on religious and funerary artefacts suggests that this may have been the case. The Hon. Sir George Bellew, KCVO, tells us that escallop shells certainly occur in armorial bearing 'almost contemporaneously with the beginning of heraldry', with the earliest known surviving examples appear on seals and in rolls of arms of seven or eight hundred years ago. So, the shell of the great scallop used as a container on the sea-witch's altar is no flight of fancy. A set of these pretty shells can be used to hold salt, bread and water and even tea lights to mark the quarters of the Circle.

There are, of course, many other kind of shells to be found on the beach and if we are really lucky there may be the rare find of a piece of mother-of-pearl – broken shells where the outer casing has been worn away, leaving the 'pearl' exposed.

Pebbles and hagstones

As Secrets of the Seashore reflects, even on a calm day, the restless shifting of stones at the sea's edge gives an indication of the tremendous forces that pile up the shingle banks. The movement of the sea continuously alters shingle beaches, and so it's worthwhile going back over old ground to see if the tide has uncovered anything interesting.

It is also worth mentioning again, the discovery of hagstones. Those found on the beaches are created naturally by the elements, or by a small, burrowing creature that works its way into the stone. Some stones are pocket-sized, while others can be the size of small rocks. Some are formed by the wear and friction of other rocks, the sea and weather, while in others a rock-boring creature called a piddock initiates the process. On south-west shores, the common piddock slowly bores holes in the rock in which it lives, by twisting itself from side to side. These molluscs can eventually erode a cliff face and by the time a piddock reaches maturity, it will have bored itself as far as a foot in depth into the rock.

Hagstones have been recorded as a protection for persons, livestock and buildings since the 17th century; the most popular use being those hung in stables to protect horses from being ridden at night by 'witches'. The hagstone is, however, an even older witches' charm for good luck and averting negative or malign energies, which should never be given away ... or any good fortune will follow it. On the other hand, if you are lucky enough to find more than one, it is a very precious gift to give to a close friend or relative.

All manner of pebbles, large and small, will be found in a sea-witch's home, acting a paper-weights and door-stops, simply because they were seen to be special, or in some way different from the rest. Many of these have been handed down through generations and it is not unusual for non-witchy people to treasure them as good luck stones even without knowing their provenance.

Do, however, be careful about what you remove from the beach for two reasons. A friend pounced with great delight on an enormous, football-sized hagstone that she found high above the water-mark on the beach. Luckily she quickly realised that the way the stone had been placed provided a perfect but unobtrusive altar in the lee of the cliff. No damage was done, but it pays to remember that you may not be the only sea-witch on the beach!

Secondly, the beach or foreshore is legally *that part of the seashore subjected to the flux of the sea, stretching from medium low tide mark to medium high tide mark, and to take away sand or shingle without permission, expressed or implied is unlawful. It is also unlawful to take away goods cast upon the foreshore from a wreck.* You have been warned.

Fossils

The beach is a good place to find fossils. In fact, some of the largest specimens in our museums have been unearthed following the collapse of a cliff face. For the sea-witch's purpose, however, the more modest finds are best suited to our needs as these still provide a *direct* link to the primordial energies we call upon in our magical workings. The remains of a dinosaur might be a bit more difficult to accommodate!

Fossils are the remains of animals or plants commonly

preserved in limestone, chalk and shale, although we must not be misled into thinking that every fossil is a remnant of an actual plant or animal. In writing about the subject in *Pebbles on the Beach*, Clarence Ellis explained that long after the creature, bone or leaf became entombed in the hardening rock, it may have decayed and finally left in the rock an exact mould of itself. Silica, carbonate of lime, or other material, which is carried in solution, then gradually filled up the space it occupied with mineral matter brought by water through the porous rock.

Again, it is the sea itself that has preserved these primordial 'still-lifes' because the rocks were slowly deposited under water, creating the ideal conditions for the preservation of organic remains. That is why the vast majority of the fossils in this type of rock are those of marine creatures. In the chalk, which was laid down in clear water, we must expect to find the remnants of organisms which inhabited such water, but in the shale, which is consolidated clay, we look for the fossils of those creatures whose habitat was muddy water.

The most common finds are graptolites (like mini fretsaw blades), trilobites (similar to a large woodlouse), brachiopods ('lamp-shells'), crinoids (fragmented stems) and ammonites (spiral shell). There are, however, innumerable other different kinds of fossils that can be found and more in-depth information can be gleaned from a basic book on palaeontology. No matter how modest the sea-witch's find, these fossilised objects can be a valuable key for focussing during meditational working.

Coloured, polished glass

Many an enthusiastic beachcomber has pounced on a piece of smoothed 'crystal', convinced they have discovered a semi-precious stone of some rarity, only to find that it is a fragment of glass, tumbled and polished by 'the rolling of thousands of tides'. Over time, a fragment of a green lemonade or brown beer bottle will have lost its sharp edges, and in the early 19th century, the lapidaries of fashionable seaside resorts made a 'brisk sale at high prices' of green, crystalline stones that were merely beach-worn pieces of old bottles!

Altar stones

On a remote beach in Wales, near the site of an old abandoned slate mine, it is still possible to find large, flat pieces of slate that have been smoothed and polished by the sea. These remnants of mined slate litter the beach and glisten like obsidian in the wet sand but once away from the water, they become dull and lifeless until they are wet again.

These make a perfect outdoor altar for a sea-witch, although others may prefer a natural niche in the rocks that is often under-water at high tide. Should you decide to remove a rock or piece of slate from the beach, remember that you are taking it away from its natural environment, and that any inland 'energies' will be different from those where the rock is bathed regularly in seawater of the natural tides.

That is why the ideal altar for the sea-witch is one that remains *in situ* among the rocks, or on a beach, where the tides act as a natural cleansing agent. If the stone (or rock) has been used by holiday-makers for a picnic spot, then wait until the tide has washed over it at least once, before using it ceremonially as part of your working.

Whim of the waves

The most unexpected magical 'gifts' can be found on the 'stran-dline', the high water line where the waves, driven by off-shore winds, deposit any debris as the tide recedes. At first glance this, more often than not, appears to be a smelly load of human junk, mixed with seaweed, but on closer inspection there could be treasure for the sea-witch to find. The most spectacular dumping occurs after a winter gale when forests of seaweed and living shells are torn from the sanctuary of deeper waters.

Marine egg-cases

Also known as a 'mermaid's purse', these are shiny oblong egg-cases with four 'horns', often ending is coiled tendrils. Narrower, yellowish ones are the egg case of dogfish; the broader, almost black kind, are those of skate. Each case would have contained a yolk about the same size as a bantam's egg, and when laid the soft tendrils would have curled around a piece of seaweed, acting as a mooring. Over the weeks of incubation the young fish develop inside the 'purse' eventually escaping through a slit at one end. These empty cases are often washed up after a storm, when they have been torn loose from the seaweed and deposited on the shore at high tide.

- Eggs are, of course, the symbol of renewal and rebirth, so any magical working involving renewal or return would benefit from being enclosed in a mermaid's purse.

- If you are lucky enough to find an egg case on the beach at a time when you intend to work a spell for the 'return' of something (i.e. health, wealth or happiness), write your wishes on a small piece of fresh paper. Tuck this inside the mermaid's purse and, weighing it with a small stone, throw it back into the sea – returning the purse from whence it came, together with your spell.

- If the purse sinks, then your request will be granted; if it floats, or is cast back onto the shore, it will be refused.

Skull of a fish or sea-bird

The skull of a fish or sea-bird can provide the sea-witch with a protective familiar of great strength if it is empowered correctly. Admittedly, this idea may not appeal to everyone but the spirit of the skull can be invoked as a Guardian, or for divinatory purposes. Skulls are fragile things and although bleached by the salt air and seawater, will require a thorough cleansing to remove any 'bits' still clinging to the bone. The best method is to keep the skull buried in dry salt for six weeks, as this will dry out and/or remove anything unpleasant, and prevent any smell.

There is also a great deal of magical lore surrounding skulls, and to find one is to receive a truly magical gift. If, on the other hand, you don't fancy the idea of taking the skull home, bury it deep in the sand near your working site above the high water mark as a form of burial ceremony for what was once another living creature.

Because of the sea's bounty, you'll rarely find a sea-witch in a New Age shop buying mass-produced tools and equipment. Even a sea-witch's knife will double-up for some practical purpose; instead of a dainty athame or a magician's ceremonial dagger, you are more likely to find them using a regulation Swiss Army knife! This thriftiness does have its practical side, simply because the salt atmosphere will soon corrode any sensitive metals and a utility-type penknife is far more useful for cutting, scraping and cleaning beach finds than a 'black-handled athame'.

Working on the sea shore

Rock pools are another result of the sea's relentless assault on the shore. This erosion has a more dramatic effect on some kind of rocks than on others, with certain rocks being worn to a lower level than their neighbours. The resulting rock pools range from a shallow basin to a deep lagoon, and each one is a complete world on its own, whether the tide is in or out. Only when the surface is perfectly calm in sheltered rock-pools does the sea give clear reflections; outside the pool the surface is broken by waves and ripples that produce a shimmer of light. It is the rock pool itself that reflects the magical adage:

As above, so below

because in the rock pool above the tide, the ocean below the water margin is encapsulated in miniature.

Of all the various seashore habitats, rock pools are the most interesting, diverse and magical. Some are teeming with marine life while others seem to contain none at all; some pools are fed by the sea, others by fresh water. Those not refreshed by every tide can even be saltier than the sea, due to evaporation. The life in the pool may not immediately spring into view: some creatures will be hidden among the seaweed, below overhanging ledges, in crevices under the rocks, or beneath loose stones. There may be tiny hermit crabs living inside winkle shells; delicate anemones; fish and prawns sheltering among the weeds and, if the pool has a sandy bottom, there may be shrimps.

Although jellyfish live in the open sea, both on the surface and at considerable depths, they often find themselves marooned on beaches, or in rock pools. In its broadest sense, the term jellyfish generally refers to 'free-swimming planktonic carnivores', that are usually transparent or translucent. They are found in most marine environments: from polar waters to the tropics; near coasts and in mid-ocean; from the surface waters to the ocean depths and are the large, often colourful, jellyfish that are common in coastal zones worldwide. Like the purple-striped jellyfish that lives off the coast of southern California and the stinging sea nettle. The latter may refer to the Atlantic or East Coast sea nettle that inhabits Atlantic estuaries; or to the Pacific or West Coast sea nettle, a common coastal species found along the west coast of North America from California to Alaska.

Of the thousands of different species, there are only about twelve recorded in British waters, the most common being the relatively harmless moon jellyfish, which is transparent with a bluish tint with four purplish rings, usually found in the English Channel and the North Sea. The compass jellyfish is also found in the Channel and although similar in shape to the moon jellyfish, it is slightly bigger and its body markings have brown and cream radiating marks on top, which resemble a ship's compass – hence the name. Occasionally, we may come across the lion's mane and the Portuguese man o'war from warmer waters, that can both inflict an extremely painful sting. Remember that even a dead jellyfish can inflict a painful wound if touched. Leave well alone but keep the image of this creature in your mind, as we will be returning to it in later chapters.

One danger that does lurk on the beach is the weever fish (*echiichthys vipera*), which moves in and out with the tide, and occasionally remains on the shore buried in the sand. On the back, near to the head, is a distinctive small spiny fin, which stands erect at the approach of any unwary paddler, and ready to sting. Although the sting is intensely painful it is not usually fatal, unless the victim has a weak heart, or happens to be a small child. The lesser weever can be found from the southern North Sea to the Mediterranean and is common around the south coast of the Britain and Ireland, the Atlantic coast of France and Spain, and the northern coast of the Mediterranean

The wound causes local considerable swelling, often accompanied by fainting, palpitations, fever, delirium, vomiting and respiratory distress. The symptoms usually subside within about 12 hours, which echoes an old fisherman's belief that the effects would last until the tide returned to the same height as it stood when the injury occurred. The recommended treatment for weever stings is to soak the area in very hot water as heat destroys the toxic qualities in the venom. It is advisable to bear this in mind, as a large number of medical people do not even know that there is a venomous fish in European waters, never mind knowing how to treat its sting.

Warning:

Overturning a stone in a rock-pool may reveal numerous creatures very different from those that live elsewhere in

the pool. They cannot survive anywhere except under their stone, nor could the creatures on the upper surface of the stone survive if it were overturned on top of them. For this reason, any stone that is moved or overturned should be replaced as quickly as possible in its former position and right side up.

Remember when examining rock pools that refraction makes submerged objects seem nearer the surface than they really are, so that what looks like a shallow rock-pool may be unexpectedly (and dangerously) deep.

Skrying in rock pools

The glare of sunshine on the sea can be painfully dazzling, but the gentle glow of moonbeams on the waves has a beautiful, calming effect. It naturally follows that using the reflection of the moon in a rock pool creates a wonderfully magical environment in which to work. Unfortunately, it is now no longer practical or safe, for a sea-witch to wander around deserted coves alone after dark to pursue his or her magical Path.

There are three alternatives and while not being ideal, each offers an opportunity to skry with seawater by the light of the moon.

Go down to the beach in the company of two or three friends on a moonlit night. One can take the opportunity for some skrying work while the others keep watch. It is much easier to work if you're not keeping half a mind on someone creeping up in the dark.

Remain on the crowded promenade and focus on the shimmering path of light created by the moon on the surface of the sea. Concentration will shut out the passers-by and you will not seem out of place or odd in staring at the sea.

Take a large container of seawater home with you and using a large dark coloured bowl, try skrying outside in the moonlight. With the right garden and atmosphere, this might be the most appropriate, especially if you don't have easy or regular access to the sea.

Whichever method you choose, empty your mind of everything else and focus on the reflection of the moon in the water and the object of your quest. Like all methods of divination, skrying will bring about different results for different people. Some may see images in the water, or on the periphery of their vision. Others may receive a response in terms of sensation or impression, rather than imagery. Remember, there is no right and wrong way, and it may also take several attempts before you manage to get on to your contacts. Skrying, like all other aspects of magic, comes easier for some than others.

No book on the subject of oceanic magic would be complete without mention of Dion Fortune's novel, *The Sea Priestess*. Whether one subscribes to the Atlantean hypothesis or not, *The Sea Priestess* lends itself to invoking the power of the sea and should be on every potential sea-witch's library shelf. Apart from being packed with 'magical truths', there is the passage that refers to the Fire of Azrael, which reveals 'the past that was dead' by 'invoking the dark Angel of the Doors that he would permit egress'.

Take two twigs of the juniper tree.
Cross them, cross them, cross them.
Look in the coals of the fire of Azrael –

According to the text, the fire of juniper boughs, interlaced with cedar and sandalwood, produces a distinctive pale charcoal of fine golden lines among the redder embers of the other woods. And according to Gettings' *Dictionary of Demons*, Azrael is one of the names of the Angel of Death, derived from the Koran; but we would be unwise to take this definition too literally, as we are not referring to the mundane levels of consciousness.

> ... *we raised a pile of juniper boughs with cedar and sandalwood mingled among them; we made it pyramidal, for that was the ancient custom ... It took the fire well, as juniper does, the flames leaping from twig to twig and throwing off the showers of sparks that characterise burning juniper; in the heart of the flame the cedar and sandal glowed with a fiercer heat and the scented smoke went rolling over the sea.*

Needless to say, even when Dion Fortune wrote her novel in the 1930s, such woods were difficult to come by, so it would be almost impossible to recreate the ritual as it was set down in the text. In *Priestess*, Alan Richardson wrote of *The Sea Priestess*: '... which stands today as the finest novel on real Magic ever written, a novel that is absolutely soaked with the rhythms of the sea to an almost hypnotic degree ...' But even if we cannot recreate Dion Fortune's magical fire, the combined salt and phosphorous in the driftwood will produce wonderful flames of red, green and blue – whether we burn the wood at home or down there on the beach at the water margin.

Le crabe enragé protection charm

One of the most common sea-creatures to be found on the beaches is the shore crab, which can be found in the highest rock pools to depths of 200 feet in the sea. In summer they move out into the brackish waters of estuaries and salt marshes, and remain higher up the shore and on mudflats when the tide drops, where they survive in small pools or burrows. These little creatures are survivalists in that they can re-grow lost limbs, and are both scavengers and ingenious predators.

This humble shore crab was once a staple part of the English diet, being shipped in large numbers to London where the poor people ate them. Elsewhere is the world, however, they have been prized as a delicacy on the tables of the rich. In Greek mythology, the crab was sent to distract Hercules when he was fighting the Hydra. The hero's foot crushed the crab, but as a reward for its efforts, Hera placed it among the stars. The zodiacal symbol of Cancer represents the crab's claws.

From a magical perspective, the Sun's entry into Cancer marks the Summer Solstice, the longest day in the northern hemisphere (in the southern hemisphere it marks the Winter Solstice and the shortest day). Shore crabs are most active at night and at high tide and are, not surprisingly, ruled by the Moon. The French name is *le crabe enragé*, and it is from the animal's habit of waving its open pincers threateningly when disturbed, that we take the image we need to use for our magical rite of protection.

- At the highest level of high tide take a small, airtight jar and fill it with seawater. [If you live inland, national newspapers give information about the tides and a brine solution can be made from Malden Salt.] This is your 'holy' water and it power is drawn direct from the sea, so there is no need for cleansing or charging.

- Now take an image of a crab, either the zodiacal symbol for Cancer, or a picture of *le crabe enragé*. If you take this from a book, magazine or newspaper, make a photocopy to prevent anything appearing on the reverse side of the image. Computer clipart would be ideal.

- If you prefer, a small piece of jewellery can be used and, once charged, will afford you the protection of the crab to carry around on your person.

If the spell is for the general protection of your home, place the image of the crab into the sea-water, and screw the jar tightly to prevent seepage. The crab represents it/you defending your quarter and, although small, it *can* pack a wallop with those pincers! Prepare the spell by moonlight, and as the image absorbs the water, visualise the crab coming alive to challenge any enemies or intruders – on both the physical and psychic levels. If the ink runs and distorts the picture, don't worry, it merely means that essence of the crab itself is entering into the water.

Allow the salt water to stand on a window sill where it can catch both sun and moonlight for seven high tides before using it to sprinkle over all the entry points to your home (including the chimney). Use whatever chant or intonation you feel comfortable with, in order to 'fix' the spell to protect against whatever you feel is a threat, or use the words:

I [Magical Name] cast this barrier of protection
around myself, my loved ones, and my home, across
which no hostile or malevolent forces dare cross.

If you are charging a pendent to wear on a chain or key-ring, then the image should remain in the seawater for the same amount of time but adapt the 'fix' accordingly. Remember that salt water is corrosive and do not use anything that could be damaged, since this would lessen the potency of the spell.

Moisture and the sea

The sea covers about 70% of the surface of the Earth, and plays a major part in the creation of our climate. Because water warms and cools much more slowly than dry land, the sea moderates temperature, making summers cooler and winters warmer than they would be on a completely dry planet.

- Ocean currents transport heat from the Equator into the high latitudes, via the warm currents of the Gulf Stream.

- The North Pole has a warmer climate than the South Pole because it lies in the middle of the Arctic Ocean, rather than in the centre of the continent of Antarctica, and there is always liquid water beneath the ice.

- Rain, snow, hail, fog, dew and frost consist of water that came originally from the sea, and returns there through rivers and ground water.

- When a tornado moves over water, it is called a waterspout. The ring of white spray at the base consists of water whipped up from the surface of the sea.

Magical tasks and exercises

Display your collection of small shells in a tall glass vase or goldfish bowl, and add to it every time you find a pretty shell. Wash the shells at regular intervals to keep them bright and clean. When only half full the bowl can still be used to hold a tea-light as part of an effective arrangement, as well as providing a focal point for magical working.

When drying driftwood for use as a staff or wand, think twice before you add any decoration. Sometimes plain is best. Make sure both are kept out of the way of curious fingers – these are magical tools and for your use only.

Try to obtain a hagstone and conceal it in a protective spot in your home. If you keep horses, a hagstone should also be kept in the stable to avert any negative intent.

Although a ceremonial knife is fine for indoor ritual, most would suffer from the elements if used on the seashore. Also remember it is an offence to carry a long-bladed knife in public, and so a good pocket-knife is an ideal solution for outdoor work.

Make sure that all your magical observations and experiences are faithfully recorded in a Magical Diary, as this will be your own personal record of an unusual journey that begins at the water's edge and leads ... who knows where.

Celebratory Rite (Outdoors)

Needless to say there is little a sea-witch can do that does not involve spending time on the seashore. Although personal safety must be paramount, it is nevertheless essential to be able to perform certain rites at the water's edge — even if there are other people about.

At the first full moon, nearest to the Spring Equinox check on the times of the high tides for that day and plan a rite to coincide with one of them. Remember that it is not considered unusual for local people to sit on the beach during the day in mid winter and for the solitary practitioner, this will be the safest measure. If you are working in a group, then it is worth considering going onto the beach after dark but do bear in mind that high tides around the equinoxes are often exceptionally *high*.

Any form of rite needs to include the 'sharing' of food and drink, even if the only participants are you and a friendly gull. Organise a picnic that can be handed out without a great deal of fuss – a lobster bisque or clam chowder in a thermos, for example, will keep the cold out. Set aside a portion of food that is to be used as an offering and give it to the gulls, using the Invocation given in the Spell Book.

If performed alone, the Invocation can be muttered as you

offer the food to the gulls without moving from the spot. If there are a number of you working out of sight in the dunes, then the Invocation can be used as part of setting up the Circle and the offering left on the beach when you leave.

Depending on the weather at the time of the Equinox, the location for the celebratory rites can be exchanged. For example, the Spring Equinox may be unbearably cold, while the Autumn Equinox could still bring summer weather.

See Celebratory Rite (Indoors).

Chapter Four

Sea Pictures

Buddha described the experience of enlightenment as 'a drop of water merging with the sea from which it came'; other mystics who have stood on the shoreline and meditated on the vast expanse of ocean, stretching to the horizon, have also reflected upon this thought. In the previous chapters, we reflected upon the practical issues of being a sea-witch – now we will take a step into the metaphysical world, and learn to look at the sea through different eyes.

From the sea-witch's perspective, we may not view the elemental powers in the same way as our inland cousins simply because ours is a different, much harsher environment. The landscape in which we work is barren and saline in comparison to the lush woods, hillsides, plains and pastures of the inland countryside, but this does not mean that our magic is any the less potent for all that. It also means that our magical correspondences will not always be in harmony with the Craft of forest and glen. As a result, the perceptions and concepts of magical working will sometimes be seen to be at odds with the more traditional forms of witchcraft.

Colour correspondences

The colour of the sea varies from a dull leaden grey in gloomy weather, or from the yellow or brown of a muddy river mouth, to a startling blue or green. Off parts of the coast, it may have a milky appearance from clay deposits and yet seen on a bright summer's day from the cliff top it may almost be a rich purple – the 'wine-coloured sea' of the Greek poets. The colour, however, is controlled by:

- the particles that float in it;
- the angle from which it is viewed;
- the brightness of the day;
- the reflection of clouds or adjacent cliffs;
- and, in the shallows, by the colour of the sea-floor.

Here, light shining through a wave crest gives a momentary glimpse of translucent green, while the billows that break on a reef are coloured by the reflection of the marine life that lives on the rocks. From *Sea & Seashore* we learn that water has a slightly bluish tint, which intercepts the reds and yellows of daylight much more quickly than the other colours, so that only the blues and greens can penetrate to any depth below the surface; a white object sinking into the water turns blue before passing out of sight.

Finely divided drops of water always look intensely white, so that the spray from a breaking wave is literally whiter than snow; compared with the spray, indeed, snow seems almost drab. In the wake left by a moving vessel the white foam contrasts with the colours of the undisturbed water, and still more strikingly with the emerald green or azure blue of the water churned up from below.

So, sea-witches working with the **Element of Water** can choose whichever colour s/he feels most appropriate for the beach on which they work. The colour correspondences for water can therefore range from pure white to muddy brown, with every shade of blue in between. And if we turn to the Table of Magical Correspondences given in *Liber 777* – we find that the colours for Water are also far ranging – from deep blue to white, flecked purple, like mother of pearl; deep olive green and sea green.

Similarly, here at the water's edge the **Element of Earth** also runs the whole gamut of colour combinations and textures, depending on the type of beach and its location. All around the coastline there are sands and shingle of every imaginable hue – purple jasper, green schist and serpentine, red and gold sand, red sandstone, yellow limestone, rock crystal, agate and carnelian – far more in fact, than the unadventurous indigo; black rayed with blue, blue-black and black as given in the Table of Correspondences.

To represent the **Elemental of Air**, what could be more fitting than a sea gull in flight, its white and blue-grey plumage contrasting with the yellow of its bill and legs, against the clear blue of the sky. Not surprising that the Table of Correspondences gives us bright pale yellow; emerald, flecked with gold; blue-emerald green; and sky blue!

And finally, what can we find on the beach to represent the **Elemental of Fire**? The Table of Correspondences gives us glowing orange-scarlet; vermilion, flecked crimson and emerald; scarlet flecked with gold, so what else can there be except the fiery sunset that reflects all these colours as the sun sinks down into the sea on the distant horizon.

A single, or combination of any of these colours, can be plaited or woven together to create the only shop-bought 'tool' (with the except of a pen-knife) in the sea-witch's armoury – the Girdle.

The Sea-Witch's girdle

To make a sea-witch's girdle, purchase several lengths of thin cord approximately nine feet long, in a combination of the colours that you feel represent the four elements. Or your own personal choice: cords may be one, two or tri- or multi-coloured. Choose the type of cord that is quite smooth and supple as there will be many occasions when you will need to wear it unobtrusively in public. Plait or twist the cords together; when the job is complete your personal Girdle should be as long as you are tall, but do not knot the cord until you are ready to empower it.

These individual cords will have been handled by people in the shop, so in order to purify it for magical use, sprinkle the

Girdle with a little Maldon salt before wrapping it in a clean, white linen napkin and secreting it away out of sight. Let it remain undisturbed for three high tides, before taking it down to the beach as the tide ebbs and shaking the excess salt into the water, letting the sea carry any negativity away.

The sea-witch's Girdle is both a magical tool and a practical one. Because the Girdle is symbolic of our own Circle of Protection it becomes imbued with powerful magical energy, which means that we can also wear it under our clothes if we feel the need to increase our magical protection. To empower the Girdle, choose a time when you can work undisturbed down on the seashore at high tide. The knots at both ends prevent it from fraying; the short tassel representing an old fertility symbol, as it is reminiscent of a bull's tassel – the bull being the form taken by Zeus when he carried Europa off into the sea. As you tie the knots at each end repeat the following:

By power of the Sea, by the old blood,
The knots are tied at the water's flood.
Woven together, I make it fast
By ancient powers of the past.
Keep me safe and free from harm,
Harken to this sea-witch's charm!
Round and about, about and around
By breaking the faith, in the waters be drowned.

You now have an extremely potent and magically charged witch's tool at your fingertips. Keep it safe but remember that you have sworn on all the ancient powers of the sea and, should that faith be broken, it would be advisable to keep well away from water in the future!

Sand dunes

Parts of our coastline with gently sloping sandy shores have wave-like ridges caused by the on-shore wind driving the sand inland. Sand dunes are great recorders of the past. Some in Britain are piled up to a depth of 50-60 feet and have buried pre-historic settlements, Roman roads, Dark Age and medieval churches – all of which have come to light again with subsequent erosion.

Among the most spectacular are those at Culbin Sands on the Moray Firth in Scotland, some of which reach 100 feet in height. Or to stand on top of the dunes at Cape Cod and watch the '*blue-black, white-toothed winter ocean climbing the sky and get sand-blasted by the long, rough wind'*. Here the winter tides and early storms tear away at the dunes, leaving a narrow margin of winter beach along the exposed cliffs.

The movement of the dunes can be more readily apparent if they are viewed in profile. Towards the wind (i.e. out to sea) there is a gentle incline, with a steep slope away from the wind. The sand is blown up the incline, and drops down on the other side, so that the dune is always moving forward, back towards the sea.

Dry blown sand around the dunes may often emit a slight or pronounced musical sound when walked over, or disturbed with a stick. Above the high-tide mark and without moisture to act as a cushion, dry grains of sand rub together when they are moved. If they are of the same shape and size, they rub against each other, vibrating and producing the 'singing' sound. These really are 'shifting, whispering sands'.

The mounds of the sand-dunes are another of Nature's way of reclaiming land, with the piles of sand being stabilised by the natural planting of marran grass, which helps check the tide's erosion. This is a plant that is so hardy that it can find nourishment even in the salty sand; spreading over the surfaces of the dunes, it protects against the wind, while its roots spread below, forming an under-lying network that binds the sand and prevents drifting.

Marran grass also fertilises the dune so that sea-spurge and sea-holly can grow, followed by lichens and bindweed. Rabbits also colonise the dunes, and they too fertilise it with organic material ... slowly the whitish sand becomes a brownish-grey soil. On the North American Atlantic seaboard, the hills and hollows behind the dunes bristle with curly 'poverty grass' and golden heather, bayberry with tiny grey-green berries and *rosa rugosa* with its big vermilion hips in the fall.

- Marran and poverty grass can also be used in spells for their protective properties: they can survive the negative aspects of Elemental Air (gale-force winds), Elemental Fire (drying heat), Elemental Water (the lack of moisture) and Elemental Earth (wind-borne salt).

- Cut the grass at ebb tide during the waning of the moon, dry it at home and use a handful on your fire as part of a banishing ritual for ridding yourself of negative forces.

As we've already mentioned, the dunes offer an excellent site for magical working, since they conceal the sea-witch from prying eyes and protect her or him from the chill wind blowing off the sea. Unless there is a convenient cave or sheltered cove in the lee of the cliffs, the dunes often afford the privacy needed for magical working. Remember, however, that a candle-flame can be seen from several miles away in the darkness, so a Fire of Azrael blazing away on the beach is an open invitation for both the interfering and idly curious.

Again, it is inadvisable to wander around the sand-dunes alone after dark. If possible, go down with two or three like-minded friends and enjoy the sensations of the night breeze whispering through the marran grass. Or lie back and test your knowledge of the circumpolar stars that have always served as a guide for mariners out on the ocean, as they complete their seasonal journey around the Pole Star.

- Shooting stars are deemed to be lucky and at certain times of the year, there are predictable meteor showers seen in the night sky. Don't forget to make a wish if you see the brief flash of a 'shooting star'.

Saltmarshes

By comparison, anyone who has grown up among the salt-marshes will tell you that these are not places to walk after dark, alone or in company. These are large, flattish tracts of mud traversed by shallow water channels, creeks and salt-pans.

On the English Romney Marshes there are abundant hardy land-plants such as sea-aster, sea-pinks, sea-lavender and common marsh grass, whose seeds are brought to it by the tide, on the wind and by birds. The growth of this vegetation checks the flow of the water and produces a further deposit of silt on to which the plants can spread. Some of the marsh may rise just above sea level and eventually become colonised by alders that can adapt quite well to brackish water. The Bay of Fundy, between the Canadian provinces of Nova Scotia and New Brunswick, has spectacular saltmarshes that extend along the 800-mile coastline.

For those who know and love the salt-marshes, however, they have their own peculiar kind of magic. Although unattractive to the average seaside visitor, they do have their own characteristic beauty, despite being dangerous and swampy. Should you have the opportunity to be taken out on the salt-marshes at night by an experienced guide, and the ground feels firm enough underfoot, allow yourself to drift away for a moment and link with the primordial swamp from which everything came. This is an extremely potent form of astral working but *never* risk it if you are alone, or you just might find yourself being pulled down into the mud on a physical level to join the 'Brown Dead Men'!

One of the most eerie features of the saltmarshes is the will-o'-the-wisp, the strange flame-like lights that are occasionally seen hovering over marshy ground. They are also known as Jack o' Lantern, Corpse Candles or, to give them the Latin name, *ignis fatuus* (*ignis* = fire; *fatuus* = foolish). Although they are now known to be caused by the spontaneous combustion of gases rising from decaying vegetable matter, for centuries they have been regarded with superstitious awe as omens of death or disaster.

There are many reasons why the saltmarshes draw people to them, irrespective of the dangers, and one is because of the large numbers of wild birds and strange plant-life that can be found there. According to *The Naturalist's Guide to the British Coastline*, almost all the plants found in the saltmarshes are 'halophytes', *hals* being the Greek word for salt. They have a specialised cell-structure and a highly adapted chemistry, which enables them not only to cope with growing in a salty substrate but also to withstand regular immersion in brine. 'They still have problems in employing a plant's normal method of osmosis to obtain water', the strategy being to take in water at times when the ground is at its least salty – during period of heavy rain, when the tide is out.

- Any dried halophtes type of plant would be useful as an ingredient in any spell summoning the strength to stand against adversity and/or difficult problems.

Birds and animal familiars
At first glance it might appear that, apart from the gulls, there are relatively few animals and birds to be seen on the seashore. Wild creatures are generally very shy and it is only the opportunists, like the gulls that show little fear of crowded summer beaches. But when the crowds have departed, either for the night or for the winter, there are all sorts of different creatures visiting the beach.

Depending on which part of the country we live, various types of animals can be seen on the shoreline. In some parts, otters and seals may be frequent visitors but even in more built-up areas it is not uncommon to see racoons and foxes hunting for crabs, or preying on nesting birds. Rats scavenge along the tide line after dark, and families of rabbits can be seen in the sand dunes at dawn and dusk.

A true witch's familiar, the natterjack toad's habitat is confined to coastal areas; it is mainly a nocturnal species, living in colonies and if there is too much disturbance in the area, then the whole colony migrates in search of somewhere more peaceful. They will announce their presence with a loud, rattling croak and can be distinguished from the common toad by a distinctive yellow back stripe. The natterjack is a species known for its longevity and can live up to its fiftieth year!

On the shores of estuaries and beaches a wide variety of sea birds exploit the different areas. Long-legged birds can wade into the water, long-billed birds probe into the mud, while shorter-legged (and usually shorter-billed) birds forage around on the beach and among the rocks, picking up food from the surface, or by turning over stones. Out at sea, fish-eating birds have perfected their different techniques for catching their food.

Raucous gulls of all kinds are never absent from beaches and harbours, and despite being the embodiment of the seaside, according to the entry in *The Penguin Guide to the Superstitions of Britain & Ireland*, gulls were traditionally thought to be the souls of seamen who had died at sea. 'Given the nature, look, and cry of the seagull', we would expect there to have been sinister beliefs about them in the distant past, but none has been found prior to the late Victorian folk-lore compilations.

The dignified blue heron, or Old Nog, as it is often called, was believed to possess a magical ability to attract fish, and can always be found in the estuaries, standing gaunt and motionless in the shallows. Some fishermen believed this power to lie in the legs, and a dead heron was quickly stripped of the skin from its shanks and mixed with the fisherman's bait, in the hope that the spell would transfer itself to him!

For those living on the Atlantic and Pacific coasts, dolphins and whales are not an uncommon sight for the sea-witch who lives by the sea. Small groups of dolphins can also be seen in British coastal waters in winter until the summer when they migrate to the Bay of Biscay for mating. At the Winter Solstice in 2003, a 'superpod' of thousands of common dolphins, stretching for more than two miles, was seen for several days off the south-west coast. Whales can be sighted in south-western waters off Land's End, having migrated northwards in spring from a warmer climate.

Although we've already mentioned encounters with dead or stranded jellyfish, the place where they come into their own is out at sea, where they appear ethereal and graceful. Some give out a brilliant white light, and at night appear as gleaming globes in the water. In fact, most kinds cannot stand bright daylight, and swim well below the surface except at night. All jellyfish sting because that is the way they catch their prey, but it should not prevent a sea-witch from admiring them as strong and beautiful swimmers, even those with a more sinister reputation. The lion's mane is brick red to brown in colour, measuring around two feet across, and is famous for its deadly part in the Sherlock Holmes story, *The Lion's Mane*; or the Portuguese man-o'-war, which is so poisonous that it is to be avoided even when helplessly stranded on a beach.

Perhaps the most magical sea-creatures of all, however, are the salmon and eels that make the arduous journeys to and from their natural spawning grounds. The eel makes its way from fresh water to breed in the Sargasso Sea in the western Atlantic (behaviour known as catadromous); the salmon feeds at sea but returns to its native river to breed (anadromous behaviour). How both the eel and the salmon manage to make these hazardous journeys, and why, is a topic that has fascinated naturalists for years. In addition to this, many rivers too polluted for other fish contain eels, and they are also plentiful in estuaries and around the coast. Eels can live out of water and they can travel overland for short distances in the autumn when the ground is wet, breathing aerated water carried in their gills.

Seeking a familiar animal

A familiar or 'totem' is a bird or animal that is associated either with your clan, family, your magical inheritance, or with a particular magical group. This concept has been part of every culture from the Stone Age throughout history, and up to the modern use of heraldry. In former times many 'clans', or tribes were named after the totem animal of their group, the clan members thus being known by a personal name together with the clan name. This can still sometimes be seen in British family names today – even though the original understanding of the name has been forgotten – e.g. Fisher (ME *fischer*, OE *fiscere*, a diriv of *fiscian* to catch fish), Ely (OE one from *æl* eel + *gē* district) or Crabbe (ME *crabbe*, OE *crabba* the crustacean).

These magical associations can be acquired or even chosen by the magical practitioner (some even using the name of an animal as part of their own magical persona). Sometimes this is recognised when an animal (or species) appears to have formed some sort of mystical link with the practitioner. For example, you might find that if you have a difficult decision to make. While walking along the seashore, you notice the unexpected daytime appearance of a nocturnal creature, or a particular animal or bird behaving out of its normal routine.

Alternately the familiar can make itself known by appearing with unusual or distinctive colouring, such as a seagull with distinctive markings or even some abnormality that singles it out from the rest. Often white or albino animals or birds are magical signs, and these might appear in meditation at the water margin, dreams, or even caught for an instant in the glare of the headlights as you drive through the inshore roads at night.

Normally, we would choose a familiar that seems appropriate either to our magical aspirations, or one with which we feel some affinity. Once the magical bond had been made, the creature will appear whenever magical questions are formed on an astral level, and any subsequent behaviour should reveal the answer.

Animal or bird familiars interact with us on a purely *personal* level, and to anyone else the sight of – for example – an exceptionally large herring gull might seem perfectly normal among the hundreds of other gulls. For the sea-witch, however, the close proximity of this piercing stare will convey the answer to his or her question. For that brief moment of time the world of the sea-witch and the gull have become one, in what we call our 'personal universe'.

Familiars do not have to be exotic creatures. In fact, a common bird or animal will be much more effective than something that excites the attention or curiosity of outsiders. Witches do not draw attention to themselves – and neither should their familiars!

Pathworking to the margin

Again we must return to the water's edge for the lead-in for this pathworking. Here we are consciously aware that although the land and sea are governed by their own supernatural lore, the narrow margin between them has long been considered a gateway to Otherworld, and as such, was dangerous place to be. In passing from the element of Earth to the element of Water, the seeker would need to act appropriately.

Barry Cunliffe addresses the reality of this elemental water margin in *Facing The Ocean* in that the power of the boundary between land and sea must always have been very real in the consciousness of those who inhabited the maritime regions. He points out that the issue was made quite explicit in a 10th century text known as the 'Colloquy of the Two Sages' preserved in *the Book of Leister*. The story tells of a young man who stood on the brink of the sea, 'for poets deemed that on the brink of water it was always a place of revelation of science. He heard a sound in the wave … so he cast a spell upon the wave that it might reveal to him what the matter might be'. As the text makes clear, the liminal region between land and sea was considered a place of communication and enlightenment.

This short extract from the John Masefield's poem, *The Passing Strange*, is perfect as a circle-casting chant, although it was obviously never intended to be used as such. There are distinct parallels within the words that certainly reflect Old Craft working and need no explanation for experienced practitioners:

Water and saltness held together
To tread the dust and stand the weather,
And plough the field and stretch the tether,

To pass the wine-cup and be witty,
Water the sands and build the city.

Be red with rage and pale with lust,
Make beauty come, make peace, make trust,
Water and saltness mixed with dust;

Now cast your Circle by marking it out in the sand with your staff. Pace the Circle while chanting the above (or by just repeating the first two lines of it), over and over, until the power has been raised. Sit down in the centre, facing out to sea, and begin to visualise a path of light leading out across the rippling surface of the water. If you can utilise the natural path of reflective light of the sun or moon then so much the better for the atmosphere for the working.

Allow your mind to travel freely until the sensation of being both within this world and without, overtakes you. For those who have experience of pathworking, the slight shift in sensation and/or perspective are the familiar signs that you are indeed on your contacts. Beginners may find the process un-nerving and lose concentration but this should not be viewed as failure – merely as being cautious, for no one should blindly follow any magical instruction without a degree of hesitation or fear.

What *no* practitioner can tell you, however, is where the pathworking will lead, for each of us follow our own path, and the one another treads will not necessarily be the same one that you follow. Remember, providing your protections are in place, no harm can befall you at this stage.

The magic of a sea cave

The creation of a sea cave is one of the natural wonders of the seashore. It begins when the erosive power of waves breaking at the bottom of the cliff exposes a natural flaw. Once a weak section of cliff has been eroded, the continuous pounding of the waves, abrasive sand, pebbles and even large rocks being hurled against it, begin to gouge out a hole in the rock formation.

Over hundreds of years, the hole increases in size and, the bigger the cavity becomes, the greater the effect of the incoming waves. The waves compress air inside the cavity to such an extent that the release of the pressure when the waves recede creates a vacuum that has an almost explosive power, shattering the surrounding rock. As the cave expands inwards, the air compressed inside by the weight of the pounding waves may produce a blowhole at the surface, sometimes a considerable distance inland.

One of the most famous sea-caves in the world, and certainly the most spectacular in Britain, is Fingal's Cave on the Isle of Staffa in the Inner Hebrides. At its mouth it is 40ft wide and 66ft tall, from sea level to roof. It also extends about 25ft down into the sea and goes back into the cliff for a distance of more than 200ft. *Fingal's Cave* – immortalised by the composer Felix Mendelssohn who named an overture after it – is aptly known as the Cathedral of the Sea.

The shape and size of a cave largely determines the sort of wildlife that can survive there, but a mature cave system, parts of which are beyond the reach of the eroding sea, is a very special place. The mouths of such caves are often protected by deep water but high inside there is often a shelf of soft sand, which remains dry even at high tide; a cave system that has a deep water entrance should only be approached by boat. This is the perfect working environment for a sea-witch but be aware that high tide can be extremely perilous if you are trapped inside with no means of escape.

Magical tasks and exercises

A visit to an army surplus store may not seem like a magical exercise, but as far as the sea-witch is concerned, the better s/he is prepared for bad weather, then the more potent and effective the magic. Even on a hot summer's evening there is always a chill breeze blowing off the sea and unless you intend to be a fair-weather witch, it is advisable to adopt the Scouting movement's motto and 'Be prepared'.

The sea-witch has no use for fancy robes and dancing barefoot in the sand, s/he is more likely to be found 'robed' in combat gear with sensible boots and thermal underwear!

Essential items
- Good walking boots with thick socks
- Rubber boots for wet weather
- A hooded parka
- Thick gloves
- Thermal underwear
- Waterproof trousers with pockets

- Army-issue waterproof, hooded sleeping bag
- Foil emergency blanket

Remember that lots of tight layers of clothing can produce a cooling effect as they prevent actual body heat from circulating. Wearing the appropriate clothing also enables the sea-witch to enjoy the beach in all weathers and at all times of the year. The sleeping bag and foil blanket comes in handy for those cold nights out under the stars with a couple of friends; tucked up snugly inside the bags means that the simple pleasure of being on the beach after dark can be enjoyed at any time ... without the cold driving you all home.

Chapter Five

Calm Sea

Even if we live some distance from the shore, it is still possible to recreate a sea-garden, especially if we are coping with poor soil conditions, since coastal plants that are regularly buffeted by howling gales and the drying effects of sea breezes, have a special kind of magic all of their own. If the garden is in full sun for most of the day with hard-baked soil, beds full of stones or rubble; or even shallow soil with rock, slate or pure chalk just below the surface, then a sea-garden might be the ideal solution.

Just because we live in an urban environment, it doesn't mean we are excluded from harnessing the magical power of the sea. A love of the sea is instinctive, even in those who have no personal or family history connected with this strange in-between world. To create a sea-garden is to re-connect with the distant shoreline on a *psychic* level, so that we are constantly aware of the power and rhythms of the natural forces, even if we are unable to experience them at first hand on a regular basis. We become like the oysters that were moved inland ... we might be a long way from the shore but we are still governed by the natural tides of our distant *spiritual* home!

As we have grown to understand, coastal plants have to cope with everything the elements choose to throw at them, with relentless spray from pounding seas and salt-laden rain, washing away the soil. Inland, however, things are less stressful and lack the harshness of coastal gardens. Coastal plants are also very different, having developed in all kinds of ways to survive, and many of the native varieties will live happily inland if they are given dry conditions, similar to those of their native habitat.

Creating a meditational sea-garden

The main ingredients for an inland sea-garden are: a site that should be in full sun for at least half of the day; various large and small rocks; an enormous amount of golden shingle (or pea-gravel); and board-walks (decking). First of all, assess what you have and decide what can be discarded and what is an asset; but don't be too hasty in removing any shrubs or trees that will destroy your privacy. If neighbouring properties offer only an unprepossessing view, erecting woven screening above the existing wall or fence height can help relieve this situation. You wish to create a garden where you can ignore the world beyond, and enjoy the benefits of your inward-looking space.

The idea is to create a garden that has an atmosphere all of its own and *very* personal. So if you have a tool shed to disguise, forget the creosote – paint it a brilliant bathing-hut yellow or candyfloss pink! On the other hand it is important to avoid the 'cluttered look', which can arise from using too many different materials. Start by deciding where your 'sitting' area will be (however small) and work outwards from there. Dig out all the perennial weeds, flatten the ground and, for the best results, use a porous membrane to cover the entire area. This often makes planting awkward but will pay dividends in the long run as it reduces the evaporation of moisture from the soil, cuts down on watering and stifles weed-growth. It also prevents gravel from disappearing into the soil.

You can never have enough gravel and if you spread it deep, it will mean you can conceal plants in their pots ... which makes it easier to move them about, and controls the spread of the roots in any invasive varieties. Most builders' merchants have different qualities of gravel and it will pay you to mooch about to see what's on offer. It can either be delivered by the lorry load, or in huge reinforced bags. Either way, unless you can have the gravel tipped straight onto the plot, you will land up with an enormous heap of the stuff at the front of the house, which then has to be moved. Nevertheless, think beach ... and be generous!

Decking is available from most DIY stores and buying with foresight, will enable you to re-position it from time to time. If you have space, a boardwalk could lead to a decking patio area for sitting out, surrounded by a sea of gravel. Choose slatted wooden garden furniture to match. Or a small town courtyard area could be set out like a chequer board, with decking and gravel making up the squares, to create visual texture all year round. Like the sea, your garden should never be static.

Garden centres now sell a variety of large rocks up to boulder size, although a monster rock would need to be allocated a permanent site on arrival. Complimentary materials like rounded boulders, timber and dressed stone can create an imaginative hard surface if blended with the right gravel and planting. And mixed materials work well together in small spaces – such as parallel flagstones laid as 'rafts' in a sea of pebbles.

As for planting, native coastal plants will survive in dry, sunny conditions, although from the sea-witch's perspective, only a few have any traditional wort-lore attached to them. What you *will* have though, is a sea-garden for meditational or magical working, even if you live miles away from the seashore.

Suggested planting

The plants listed here are those suitable for northern European gardens and will not always be suitable for the warmer climates of, say, California or Florida. American books such as *Old Time Herbs for Northern Gardens* by Minnie Watson Kamm, suggest that many of the plants mentioned here would be compatible with gardens in the northern States, many having been taken from Europe by the early settlers. Local garden centres can advise on the appropriate planting for the area in which you live.

Ornamental grasses: Found all around our shores, marram grass *(ammophila arenaria)* binds the dunes together with its knotted root-stock. The blade-like stems curl to protect the leaves from the sun and wind, and open flat when it rains. Like poverty grass, this would prove too invasive for a garden and so it is better to use other plants to replace these native ones, as there are many that will enhance the inland sea-garden. For example: blue lyme grass (*leymus arenarius*) is known as a classic seasider with silvery uprights and pale biscuity heads of corn; or *festuca glauca*, with its spiked mounds of needles; *stipa arundinacea* creates olive and orange fountains, and the fluffy *stipa tenuissima* that dances gently in the breeze. There is also the spectacular black Mondo grass (*ophiopogon planiscapus nigrescens*) that sports heads of purple flowers in the summer. To prevent them all from spreading out of control, plant in clumps in their pots at the edge of the decking to soften the straight lines of the wood, and keep well-watered.

Thrift (*armeria maritima*): A common garden plant, also known as sea pink, that grows in low, dense tussocks that keep the roots of the plant shaded from the sun. It is found growing naturally on the rocks and cliffs of the seashore and flowers from April to August. Also known as the 'plant of sympathy', it was featured on George VI brass three-penny bits and although it has no medicinal value, it has been trans-planted into inland gardens since at least the 15th century. Ideally placed at the foot of large stones, or planted in any cracks or crevices in the stone.

Sea kale (*crambe maritima*): A striking plant found along the southern shores of Britain, whose leaves are coated with a waxy substance to protect them from the sun and winds. The new shoots are purple and later short stocky stems shoot out, covered with small, sweetly-scented white flowers. It is a native perennial found on the coastal shingle, sand and rocks, often at the tide line. It was once a highly prized vegetable; the shoots being fried in breadcrumbs and doused with lemon juice, or served with toast and lashings of butter. Flowers from May to August.

Horned poppy (*glaucium flavum*): Found on seashores all around Britain, it has thick hairs on the upper-side of the leaves to protect them from the sun. Its yellow satiny flowers eventually produce seedpods that fling the new seeds out into the shingle. The plant produces an orange-coloured sap that smells unpleasant but was once used in the treatment of bruises. Flowers from June to September.

Sea holly (*eryngium maritinum*): A spectacular seaside plant with leaves heavily armed with sharp spikes. Even the blue flowers and the seeds that follow them are prickly. Sometimes the native variety is hard to grow but many other closely related species will thrive. The roots of the sea holly candied with sugar and orange flower water were used as an aphro-disiac, particularly by older men. Falstaff mentions it in *The Merry Wives of Windsor*. Once used to flavour jellies and toffee or made into a conserve. Can be taken internally for urinary infections. Flowers from July to August.

Sea buckthorn (*hippophae rhamnoides*): A deciduous highly ornamental shrub with silvery needles and orange berries that often grows big enough to protect other plants from the weather. A shrub found on most British coasts but native only in the east. Often planted to stabilise dunes, the females flower from March to May and fruit in September. The berries are seen at their best in November, especially in the early sunlight after a night of frost. These are used to make into jelly or sauce as an accompaniment to fish dishes, although unpalatable when raw.

Tamarisk (*tamarix gallica*): Was introduced into Britain during Tudor times and regarded as a *'sovereign remedie against the great and undurate passion of the spleen'*; while others mention its use in treating *'disordered livers and hard spleen'*. It can grow up to 12 feet high and has spectacular sprays of white flowers tinged with pink in the late spring. It grows from cuttings as readily as willow and, like willow, was used for making lobster pots.

Burnet rose (*rosa pimpinellifolia*): The stems of this plant are short and bristly with large creamy-white flowers with bright-yellow stamens. It is fairly common around the coast, except in the south-east. Flowers May to July and produces distinctive purple-black hips during August and September, which can be used to produce rose-hip syrup, a rich source of vitamin C.

Rosa Rugosa (*rosa rugosa*): Also known as the hedgehog or Japanese rose, is a vigorous dense species with purplish-red flowers, wrinkled leaves and large, vermilion hips. Flowers in the summer and autumn in the shelter of the dunes. Listed as an aromatic tonic herb; the hips being a source of vitamin C.

Heather (*ericaceae*): Many species and colours of heather can also be found in the shelter of the dunes. Most are evergreen and the hardy varieties have an extended flowering period that give good ground cover. Some of the best honey is made from heather blossom and the whole plant has a wide range of medicinal uses.

Sea lavender (*limonium vulgare*): Flowers on sand-dunes and muddy sea shores from July to November in a profusion of purple blooms, although it is not particularly easy to grow out of its own natural habitat. Common on some English coasts, but rare elsewhere and absent in Ireland and north Scotland. The flowers are often dried and used for decoration in winter; our ancestors used the seeds as a remedy for dysentery.

Samphire (*crithmum maritimum*): A strongly aromatic, salty herb that has a diuretic effect, cleanses toxins and improves digestion. Leaves are eaten in salads, cooked in butter, or pickled. Needs well-drained soil and a warm, sheltered position. Although it grows wild on cliffs and coastal paths, it needs protection in cold winters.

Monbretia (*crocosmia x crocusmiiflora*): Monbretia is a foreign import that has naturalised on our cliff-tops. They colonise well and provide huge sprays of bright orange flowers from July to August. No culinary or medicinal use but ideal for corner planting.

Lavender, rosemary, thyme: Plus many other highly scented Mediterranean natives will survive quite happily in a sea-garden environment. A wide range of herbal plants would suit a baking hot, very dry bed that is exposed to the sun all day, providing they are watered well at night. It is all a question of selecting the right plants for the conditions to produce a garden full of the aromas of the Mediterranean. These herbs have more culinary and medicinal uses than the rest put together, and can be found listed in any herbal.

Warning:

Although you can remove large interesting pebbles or rocks, and driftwood, from a beach, it is illegal to remove plants from the shore-line; it would also be cruel to remove sea creatures from their natural environment as they will quickly die.

Reflect for a moment

In very small gardens everything counts. Meticulous planning is essential over how we intend to use the space, and what we wish to have in it. When room is restricted, the design of that space becomes all-important, although *A Witch's Treasury for Hearth & Garden* tells us that a canny witch will utilise every nook and cranny for growing things even if we don't have so much as a patio or yard.

Even a small space can give a witch space to 'be' and your neigh-bours will think nothing if they see you sitting on the step with a coffee, or relaxing in a garden chair in your special corner. Being a witch doesn't mean that you have to make grand ritual gestures to follow your beliefs – a quiet corner prepared with loving care is the only sacred space you need

But before dashing off to the local garden centre, mark the four cardinal points – or quarters – using a compass. Remember, if its big enough to sit in, it's big enough to use magically, so think about how you can create a meditational area that will mean nothing to any inquisitive over-lookers. And before you decide that wind-chimes made from sea shells would be perfect for representing Elemental Air, be warned that a couple were threatened with prosecution when local authority officials ruled that their wind chimes were causing noise pollution, following complaints from the neighbours!

To make it personal, every garden needs a 'conversation piece' that is not a mass-produced purchase from the local garden centre. The sea-witch should be on the look-out for unusual items such as an old-fashioned lobster pot, coloured glass fishing floats, a large piece of driftwood, a ship's lantern, bell or wheel, etc. A friend once lugged home a huge, painted figurehead from an old ship that had long before gone to the breakers' yard, but it now has pride of place in the garden, despite its hideous and disagreeable countenance! Strategically placed, these items can add their own little bit of sea-magic to an urban garden.

Also take into account that if the garden is in full sunlight all, or most of, the day, it will be unbearable to sit in unless you provide yourself with some form of artificial shade. Think 'seaside' and go for one of those really large colourful garden umbrellas, or a bright, retractable awning. Both also give the added advantage that you can still sit outside, even when it's raining!

Ritual for dedicating a meditational garden

Calculate a time when it is high tide nearest to where you live, and light a candle in a suitable container – a storm lantern, or one that will shelter the flame from the wind as the ritual must be performed outside. For this you will need:

- A blue candle
- A large sea shell
- A small jug of sea-salt brine
- A suitable charm, or piece of 'sea' music.

For example, Benjamin Britten's *Four Sea Interludes* is a superb presentation of the sea in many moods and lasts for 16¼ minutes, which is ample time for a dedication.

Place the shell to your ear and listen to the sound of the waves murmuring on some distant shore. Visualise your favourite beach while you listen to the music, or quietly recite to yourself the full version of John Masefield's poem, *Sea Fever*, the following being the second verse:

I must go down to the seas again, for the call of the running tide
Is a wild call and a clear call that may not be denied.
And all I ask is a windy day with the white clouds flying;
And the flung spray and the blown spume, and the sea-gulls crying.

This extract from the poem echoes the purpose of a charm, in that it becomes a wish to return to the seashore visualised in your mind's eye. Sprinkle your brine (made from sea-salt, or sea water previously collected for magical purposes) in the direction of the four points of the compass, and respond to the *'wild call and a clear call that may not be denied'*. If the tides are right, you may receive a sign that a psychic link with the seashore of your visualisation had been established.

The Beaufort Scale

As we have seen earlier in the text, witches have long been credited with having control over the weather and the magical ability to raise storms at sea. One suspects that they were merely more canny in reading the signs that bad weather was on the way, and exploited their neighbours' gullibility for their own ends. A lot of magic relies on illusion and an accurate prediction concerning approaching storms would have increased many a witch's stock-in-trade a hundredfold in the community. A rustle of wind in the trees and cloud formation would provide all the information s/he needed to know about how the weather would react within the next few hours.

In 1808, Admiral Sir Francis Beaufort, Hydrographer to the Navy (1829–55) put things on a more formal footing and devised a system that was used to define wind force. The Beaufort Scale showed how wind speeds (in miles per hour) could be roughly estimated from fairly simple observations. For example, see table below.

Force 12 is a hurricane, with wind speeds of 73–82 mph, but the scale now goes up to Force 17 (126–136 mph) and suddenly, we get a much clearer picture of what made that 'jumble of words' in the shipping forecast (Chapter One) so important. The sea-witch, sitting comfortably in her inland meditational garden, can watch the smoke rise leisurely from her neighbour's chimney and *know* that the distant sea is calm with a mirror-like surface.

When winter storms rip slates from the roof of the house opposite, she can visualise the grey sea beginning to 'roll' with the flying spray reducing visibility, and adapt her magic accordingly.

Land Observations	Sea Observations	Wind Speed	Force	Description
Smoke rises vertically	Sea like a mirror	Less than 1	0	Calm
Light drift of smoke	Light ripples	1–3	1	Light air
Wind felt on the face, leaves rustle	Small wavelets, no foam on crests	4-7	2	Slight breeze
Leaves in motion. Wind extends light flag.	Large wavelets, crests begin to break	8-12	3	Gentle breeze
Wind raises dust and small pieces of paper. Small branches of trees move.	Small waves, frequent white horses	13-18	4	Moderate breeze
Small trees in leaf begin to sway; crested wavelets on inland waters.	Moderate waves; chance of some spray	19-24	5	Fresh breeze
Large branches in motion. Whistling in telegraph wires.	Large waves and spray	25–31	6	Strong breeze

Whole trees in motion. Difficulty in walking against the wind.	Heavy seas with foam from breaking waves blown in the direction of the wind.	32-38	7	High wind
Twigs break off trees	High waves and foam blown in streaks.	39–46	8	Gale
Chimney pots and slates blown off some houses.	Sea begins to 'roll'. Spray may affect visibility.	47-54	9	Strong gale
Trees uprooted and severe structural damage. Seldom experienced inland.	High waves covered in foam, and poor visibility because of spray.	55-63	10	Whole gale
Widespread structural damage. Rarely experienced.	Exceptionally high waves. Sea covered in long white patches of foam.	64-72	11	Storm

Sea-Magic at home

With the right aids or tools, there is very little magic that the sea-witch cannot perform at home. Even if that home is far from the seashore. By utilising the jars of mud, sand and seawater, the driftwood staff, and the growing collection of shells and shore-gathered pebbles, we have all the 'props' (in the theatrical sense) we need.

Providing we have created a suitable space from which to respond to the *'wild call'* of the ocean, we can create our seashore in our mind's eye at any time, just as experienced, ritual magicians often work solely from an astral temple. Once we've sprinkled our seawater in the direction of the four points of the compass and, if we've done our homework on local tides, we can re-establish the psychic link with the seashore of our visualisation.

To prepare for a magical working, adapt the formula given for dedicating the sea garden. In other words, calculate a time when it is high tide nearest to where you live, light a candle in a storm lantern and place it outside. Light this lantern on nights when you're *not* working, and your neighbours won't take any notice when you *are* engaged in something more serious. For this you will need:

- Two appropriately coloured candles
- Perfumed joss or incense
- Sand
- Sea water
- A suitable charm (see Chapter Eight)

As well the harnessing the power of the natural tides, for magical purposes (i.e. spell casting), we also have to take other elements into consideration. Certain days of the week are appropriate for certain actions, and each has its own attributes. Some basic examples are as follows:

Sunday: (*Planet – Sun; Colours – yellow, gold*)
All things pertaining to personal advancement, ambition, finances.

Monday: (*Planet – Moon; Colours – white, silver, pearl*)
All things pertaining to domestic concerns and psychic matters.

Tuesday: (*Planet: Mars; Colours – red, orange*)
All things governed by dynamic action, confrontation, ambition.

Wednesday: (*Planet: Mercury; Colours – green, silver, magenta*)
All things related to communication, correspondence and social activity.

Thursday: (*Planet: Jupiter; Colours – purple, blue*)
All things relating to business matters, expansion and material wealth.

Friday: (*Planet: Venus; Colours – pink, pale green*)
All things relating to relationships, romantic love and social activities.

Saturday: (*Planet: Saturn; Colours – black, indigo, brown*)
All things relating to Time and endurance.

Magical rituals are extremely personal, and although it is permissible to use those given in 'spell books', those we create for ourselves will be far more potent – and have far more meaning for us. Rest assured that the majority of 'published' spells will have been created especially for inclusion in that particular book purely as examples – *they are not the charms the author will be using in his or her own Circle!* Use those included in the text as pointers, by all means, but don't be afraid to experiment and create spells of your own. If we constantly bear in mind the basic rules of magic, we can do almost anything we choose.

A typical magical working should be constructed as follows:

Type of ritual
Understand *what kind* of magical working we are initiating.

Purpose of the ritual
It is essential to have a very *clear idea* of what we wish to achieve.

Ritual preparation
Any magical working must be *planned in advance* so no mistakes are made. Attempting to cast a spell without planning is asking for trouble.

Cast the Circle
Visualise yourself contained within a bubble of shimmering, blue light that *cannot be breached*.

Invocation
Call upon the appropriate spirits or entities that are *relevant* to that particular working.

Statement of intent
The repetition of the purpose of the ritual is important, and must be carried out with *sincerity and conviction*.

Actual working
The power raised in the working is contained within the Circle *until it is released*, or directed towards its goal.

Thanking the spirits or entities
Although we raise the energy within ourselves, we are thanking the 'powers that be' for the added oomph, and *acknowledging the existence* of a power greater than our own.

Closing the Circle
Close the Circle by visualising the bubble shrinking by breathing it back in through the nostrils. When the energy has completely dispersed, we allow ourselves a quiet moment to *'earth'* ourselves.

For the purpose of this exercise, we will imagine that we are attempting to heal a rift between family members. Because there are always two sides to a quarrel, we must put aside all *personal* involvement (as difficult as this may be), and not allow our feelings to influence our judgement.

- We must get our timing right.

- Because we wish to dissipate the anger, we will need to calculate when the local tide will be ebbing, not at the actual turn of the tide, but somewhere in between.

- Because Friday/Venus governs relationships, the working would best be performed seven hours after high tide on that day.

- If the moon is waning, so much the better.

The purpose of the spell and the ritual preparation go hand in glove. Writing down the words we wish to use during the working can ensure we have a clear idea of what we wish to achieve, and eliminate the risk of a mistake. The words can be recited aloud, or silently consigned to the candle flame. We must also take into account that magically forcing someone to go against their own interests or inclinations (i.e. returning to a violent partner) is **black magic**, whether we like to admit it or not!

Hopefully, you can unobtrusively utilise your sea-garden setting for casting the Circle and marking the quarters by using sand (North-Earth); rose or carnation perfumed joss (East-Air); pink or green candle (South-Fire) and seawater (West-Water). The colour of the candles and the joss corresponds to Venus-Friday, which governs relationships. Even sitting in a garden chair, you are safely encased in your protective bubble and can begin to raise the spell-power ... first by summoning the spirit/entity to energise the working. Try to hold the image of waves pounding on the beach in your mind, as you repeat over and over the charm that will 'fix' the spell and carry it through to its conclusion. Use the power of the waves to build up the power of the charm.

Keep repeating the charm until you feel a sudden lightness, or some other sensation, that tells you the spell has gone home. Let the waves begin to recede as the tide falls back, leaving piles of seaweed at the high tide mark. As the sea grows calm, the spirits/entities are thanked and dismissed, before you close the Circle. To the casual observer, you would just be sitting in your garden, lost in thought, with a couple of candles about, and perfumed 'stuff' to keep the insects at bay!

If we were working this spell on the seashore, we wouldn't need to visualise the power of the ocean because it would be there in front of us in all its glory. Working from home requires the added complication of having to visualise at the same time as raising the power, *and* concentrating on the wording of the charm. With practice, however, it can be done, and your spells will be more successful because of the additional discipline. Your sea-garden also gives that added advantage by creating the right atmosphere and because it is your own sacred space.

Jewels from the deep

- **Pearls** of any value are usually found in warm waters but some British shellfish produce tiny ones. In fact, British river pearls from freshwater mussels were known to the Romans.

- **Coral** used for making jewellery belong to the genus *Corallium* and are well known for their spectacular delicate red or pink skeletons. *C. rubrum*, the species found in the Mediterranean, has been collected by man since Neolithic times. The Romans used to grind it to a powder, which was taken as medicine, and in the Middle Ages is was believed to possess various magical properties.

- **Jet** is fossilised wood washed out of the 'jet bed' on the British coast. It can still be picked up on the North Yorkshire coast in the shape of dark pebbles, rolled and worn to dullness. If rubbed it will attract small pieces of paper, etc but its brilliance can only be achieved by cutting and polishing.

- **Amber** can be picked up in small pebbly lumps on shingle beaches. It burns with a pale flame and has a pleasant, aromatic odour. The dull surface will not suggest the rich yellow of amber but if it is rubbed, the resulting 'electrification' will attract hairs, paper, etc. The ancient Greek word for amber is *elektron* – the basis of our own word electricity.

- **Obsidian** is an almost black, glassy rock that cooled too quickly from its molten state. Obsidian stones (resembling bottle glass) can occasionally be found on the beaches of eastern England, to which they were transported by glaciers. In America it is often referred to as 'Apache tears'.

Magical tasks and exercises

Magical correspondences
All areas of magic require a knowledge and understanding of magical correspondences if the working is to be successful. The following are traditionally associated with Elemental

Water and although we have already looked at the wide range of sea colours, for the purpose of this exercise we will use here only the basic correspondences for Water.

Spirits/Entities: Poseidon; Neptune; nymphs, undines, nereids

Colours: Deep blue; white flecked purple (like mother of pearl); deep olive green; sea green;

Precious Stones: Beryl; aquamarine; pearl

Flora: Lotus; all water plants

Fauna: Eagle; snake; scorpion

Magical Aptitude: Crystal gazing; preparation of talismans

Perfumes: Onycha [an extraction of shellfish! now rare], myrrh

Zodiac: Cancer; Scorpio; Pisces

Tarot: The Hanged Man

Chapter Six

The Roaring of the Wave

Because of the inherent dangers and uncertainty of the sea, it is advisable to have an understanding of its darker side. And nowhere is this 'dark side' more apparent than in accepting that although many sailors are nominally Christian in their beliefs ashore, many still instinctively pay homage to the old pagan gods when they are at sea. In fact, many still use 'magic and ritual' in the form of superstitious or traditional gestures, to protect themselves against the treacherous forces of nature, and respect the same powerful superstitions as their ancestors did.

Sooner or later, the sea-witch will want to put to sea, but should not forget that the boats themselves are also an integral part of sea-lore. According to *Folk-lore, Myth & Legend of Britain*, from the moment the keel of a new boat was laid, tradition and superstition guided the boat-builder's hand. To complicate matters further, certain types of wood were considered to be lucky and at one time, no boat would have been considered seaworthy unless some part of it was made of rowan, ash or some other 'lucky' wood.

In the 19th century, Scottish fishermen also believed that some woods were male and others female, and that a boat of female wood sailed faster at night than during the day. She-oak, or chestnut, was thought to have this quality.

To protect the boat and its future occupants, boatyard superstitions were scrupulously observed. It was considered disastrous to begin work on a new craft on a Friday and to counteract any accidents, the boat-builder would often tie a red ribbon around the head of the first nail he used. For added protection, a gold coin was built into some hidden recess within the framework, and it is still customary for a silver coin to be placed underneath the mast. Contrary to many landlubber's superstitions, the magical properties of iron were highly prized and it was not unusual for a horseshoe to be nailed up in the deckhouse, or on the mast. And as we know, in the Mediterranean, an eye is painted on the bow of a ship to ward off the 'evil eye'.

The carved figurehead was believed to bring good luck and gave the vessel a unique appearance, so other ships could identify it, and many were the work of woodcarvers who specialized in creating these awesome images. These wood-carved figures were also popular with nautical equipment suppliers, outfitters, instrument makers, and sail makers, who also used them to promote their wares to the crews when in port ... some of the figures were carved by the sailors themselves.

Needless to say, ritual and superstition surround the actual launching of a boat, as we can see when a large ship is 'christened' with a bottle of champagne being smashed against its bows. In Scotland, fishermen taking charge of a new boat will use whisky for the same purpose ... or rather than sacrifice a good malt, barley can be sprinkled over the bow ... they also believe that a boat should only be launched when the tide is flowing, and that no vessel should be named until it is afloat.

In fishing communities, the luck of the fishing boats was renewed each year at Christmas or the New Year by carrying fire around them in the harbour. This protective measure was said to ward off ill-wishing or negative energies, while on a daily basis many fishermen observed their own personal rituals before setting sail. Like touching the bow first thing in the morning, spitting over the side, or spitting on a coin before throwing it overboard. 'To the casual observer, such actions may appear to be prompted by private superstitions; but in fact, they are part of a nationwide pattern of custom and belief, like the landsman's habit of touching wood for luck.'

If sea-witches decide to extend their world beyond the boundaries of the water margin, then it may be fortuitous to take some of these old superstitions in to account. Not because we should allow superstition to cloud our judgement but because those who live by and on the sea, are always mindful of the supernatural energies of those surging waters.

Our Britain ancestors have a long history of boat building: vessels consisting of separate planks being lashed together, can be traced back to the earliest finds from around 1600BCE. Parts of three or four vessels found on the Humber estuary and the remains of another found in the River Dour at Dover are from about 300 years later. All were built of oak planks, fastened with lashings of yew, although a later find - the so-called Brigg 'raft' - dating to around 800BCE from a tributary of the Humber, had a continuous stitching of willow. Although archaeologists maintain these designs are river vessels (which would be difficult to handle at sea), it does not rule out the likelihood of there being plank-built sea-going ships built around the same time.

It is also incongruous to believe that our ancestors would have launched a boat and put to sea, without some propitiatory rites being performed to keep the ship and its crew free from harm. The customs of a sea-faring people would have been an oral tradition and many of the enduring superstitions still observed by sailors, may have their roots in these early boat-building communities. How many of these customs were carried to America aboard the Mayflower?

For modern sailors, however, there are still dozens of taboos that govern the speaking of certain words, gestures or encountering certain animals or types of people before setting sail. The greatest maritime fear, however, is of drowning. One old superstition claimed that if a sailor rescued a drowning man, he would probably be drowned himself, for attempting to cheat the sea of its due. 'It was this belief that gave earlier generations of seamen their fatalistic acceptance of drowning and a reluctance to help those in trouble; and very few ever learnt to swim.'

One well-known seafarer's amulet that was said to protect against drowning was the acquisition of a caul – a membrane that cover some babies' heads at birth. The baby born with a caul was thought to be particularly lucky, and so long as the caul remained in its possession the owner would never drown. The protection could be transferred, and well into the 20th century, sailors would still pay as much as £20 for one.

So ... if we are going to put to sea, there are one or two obser-vances we will need to make before getting afloat, especially when buying a boat. All boats have to come out of the water for a survey, or yearly for cleaning ... do not let the vessel go back in the water without performing your own propitiatory rites in the form of circling the boat with an appropriate 'element balancing' incense. Echo the launching of the fishing boats with the following 'blessing':

O thou Serpent of old, Ruler of the Deeps,
Guardian of the Bitter Sea, Prince of the
Powers of Water, be present we pray thee and
guard this boat from all perils of the Sea.

Sailor's craft

As we realise, a sailor's life under sail was both arduous and perilous, and yet there were slack periods during which they turned their hands to intricate carving, rope-work and scrimshaw to relieve the boredom. During the long days at sea, sailors passed the time by developing these skills, which could be sold when they went ashore. Examples of these crafts are displayed in nautical museums, and often demonstrate tremendous attention to detail in the intricate and ingenious designs of simple every day items. Sea-witches can familiarise themselves with these tradi-tional crafts and utilise them in working the magic of the seashore for spell-casting and protective amulets.

Macramé is a form of textile-making using knotting rather than weaving or knitting. Its primary knots are the square knot, and forms of hitching (full hitch and double half-hitch) that have been used by sailors, especially in elaborate or ornamental forms, to decorate anything from knife handles and bottles, to parts of ships. They made macramé objects at sea to be sold or bartered when they landed; 19th-century British and American sailors making hammocks, bell fringes, and belts, using 'square knotting' after the knot they used most.

When we think of macramé today, we tend to refer to decorative plant-holders and other handicrafts, although the craft (also known as Chinese Knotting), is very ancient, with artefacts dating back thousands of years. We rarely associate the term macramé with nautical knotwork today, and yet the tying of knots and making ornamental rope designs was the sailors' only form of relaxation during their leisure time on long voyages under sail.

There are dozens of books available on the subject and if this type of handiwork is in your line, then you will have hours of pleasure in creating or decorating your own ritual 'tools' in this manner. Like all things in Craft, however, knotwork can also be used for more magical purposes, and often crop up in historical reports of witch-magic. Take for example:

The Curse of Nine
Ane's name
Twa's some
Three's a pickle
Four's a curn
Five's a horse-lade
Six'll gar his back bow,
Seven'll vex his breathe
Aught'll bear him to the ground
And nine'll be his death.

This traditional 'ladder' begins with a small affliction and finishes with death itself. The repetitive chant of such cumulative magic would be mumbled under the breath as each knot was securely tied. The knotted cord would then be concealed about the property of the one cursed and allowed to work its magic - unless the 'ladder' could be found and the knots untied, the spell would run its course. The more involved the knotwork, the less chance there would be of unravelling it *in reverse order to which the knots were originally tied*!

Should the matter require less drastic measures, we can use a familiar binding spell to prevent someone carrying out some action that is not in *their* best interest. Ideally, this working requires an object link with the person at whom the binding is aimed, and this should be plaited into a triple cord with red twine. Take the cord in the left hand and tie nine knots in it, starting with one at either end and working inwards. As the knots are tied, visualise the person for whom the spell is intended and begin the chant:

[Name ...] *I conjure thee,*
By night your eyes are blinded!
By clay your ears are stopped!
By earth your mouth is sealed!
By rock your limbs are bound!

Having tied the ninth knot, end with 'So mote it be!' and carefully bury the cord in the ground. Once the spell has achieved its ends, the cord can be unbound by untying the knots *in reverse order to which they were originally tied*. Beginning with the centre knot, and chanting as you go, visualise the magical bonds falling away ...

By winds your limbs are freed,
By the breath your mouth is opened,
By the word your ears are opened,

By the light your eyes are brightened.
[Name ...] I conjure thee,
Awake, arise; so mote it be!

Binding is a form of preventative magic inasmuch as the spell can be used to stop someone doing something foolhardy – such as taking out a loan they can ill-afford; running off with the window-cleaner; or making an ill-advised confession! It is not meant to be permanent and, unlike cursing or 'bottling' should be easily reversed when the moment of madness has passed.

As we can see, the **Witch's Ladder** is a cunningly simple device, and easy to make, yet indispensable for spell working, because it allows us to keep a count of the number of repetitions a chant or charm had when it was cast. The simplest method is just a length of plain cord with knots tied in it at regular intervals. Or special length of ornamental cord can be put aside for impromptu magical working ... ready to hand, should the need arise.

Decide beforehand how many repetitions the charm should have, then simply tie the equivalent number of knots into the cord. For example, a traditional weather charm for wind has three knots two on the outside, the third (and last one to be tied) in the centre. And *'as these knots are loosed, so mote the weather be!'* When we begin the charm, we run the cord through our fingers, moving onto a new knot for each repetition.

Most people will remember **Cat's Cradle** as a popular playground game that involves two or more players in creating a web of string that could be passed from hand to hand. What many *don't* realise is that cat's cradle is probably one of humanity's oldest games, and is spread among an astonishing variety of cultures from the Arctic to the Equatorial zones. Although not a nautical pastime, the Cradle is perfect for focussing the mind should two or three of you wish to produce a *permanent* binding spell.

As with the game, the spell begins with the first player wrapping a loop of string around the hand and taking one side of the string and circling the hands again. The aim of the game/spell is to make a series of figures including the 'cat's cradle'. The basic moves are very simple and is always started with the above opening. After that each participant pinches the x's and wraps them around the outside strings, passing the cradle from person to person. Other moves tend to be more complicated and need a little more practice.

The cradle is best used if there is to be no 'release', since at the end of the charm, the string is pulled free and there is no way of reversing it. Using the first line of the charm will set the spell in place; each subsequent line representing one person's move in creating another 'layer' in the spell. Repeat as necessary and when the cradle is complete, pull the string free to 'fix' the spell.

Remember, however, that 'binding' someone against their will (or keeping them bound to something or someone that is against their best interests) *is black magic,* **no matter what excuse is given by the person requesting the spell to be cast. This type of magic has a nasty habit of rebounding on the sender, so no binding, bottling or cursing spells should be set in motion without a considerable amount of forethought and conviction. Bear in mind that any rebound will return to the person sending the spell, not the person requesting it!**

Scrimshaw is the name given to handiwork created by whalers, and was most commonly made out of the plentiful supply of bones and teeth of whales, and the tusks of walruses. It took the form of elaborate carvings in the form of pictures and lettering on the surface of the bone or tooth, with the engravings highlighted, or small sculptures made from the same material. The making of scrimshaw began on whaling ships between 1817 to 1824 on the Pacific Ocean, and survived until the ban on commercial whaling.

The earliest authenticated pictorial piece of scrimshaw (1817) is a whale's tooth inscribed with the following: *This is the tooth of a sperm whale that was caught near the Galapagos Islands by the crew of the ship Adam [of London]...'* Other sea animal ivories were also used as alternatives for whale teeth; walrus tusks, for example, may have been acquired in trade from indigenous walrus hunters. Most accessible pieces today will either be in family collections, or found in antique shops ...but if you decide to buy remember the old magical adage of not haggling over a black egg!

Scrimshaw was essentially a leisure activity for whalers. Because the work was dangerous at the best of times, whalers were unable to work at night and this gave them a great deal more free time than other sailors. A lot of scrimshaw was never signed and so a great many of the pieces are anonymous. Early scrimshaw was done with crude sailing needles, and the movement of the ship, as well as the skill of the artist, produced drawings of varying levels of detail and artistry. Originally candle black, soot or tobacco juice would have been used to bring the etched design into view.

Needless to say, any scrimshaw that comes into our possession will be old, since whales are now protected species and the supply of 'ivory' has almost ceased. If a piece does come into our hands, rather than being repelled by the idea of owning an item made from a by-product of whaling, we should look upon it as a sacred trust. This was once part of a creature from the Deep, and that part of it lives on, in the guise of a rare and precious sea-witch's amulet.

Unlike other sea-finds, something man-made and as old as this, will have been through many hands before it comes into the 'safe harbour' of the sea-witch's possession, and will need to be thoroughly cleansed of all negative influences before it can be magically charged.

For the sea-witch such items can be used to provide talismans and amulets, either for personal use or to give away. Any other seashore finds, such as bone, mother-of-pearl or animal teeth can be utilised and engraved with suitable nautical or magical sigils. To consecrate and empower the object for your particular purpose, hold the flaked or broken off pieces in one hand and the cleansed object in the other, and plunge your hands up to the wrists in sea-water. Release the pieces back into the sea and allow the water to wash through your fingers to empower the amulet, while you focus your mind on the purpose of the amulet/ talisman.

Generally speaking, a talisman is a protection *against* something, while an amulet is a power-object for *attracting* good fortune. Each piece should be kept in its own protective pouch in order to prevent the energies from becoming contaminated by other items, even if they are magical tools.

Woodcarving was another popular sailor's pastime and some of these objects are now to be found on the antiques market. We are familiar with ships' figureheads but as we have seen, there were also smaller items that sailors carved during their voyages – often made from woods such as rosewood and mahogany. The craft of painting and carving wood reached the peak of its popularity during the 17th and 18th centuries, and foreign ports of call gave sailors a rich place to pick up more exotic types of timber.

Working with wood is a craft in itself and admittedly, not all of us have the ability to create beautiful objects out of timber. What we can produce, however, are small amulets and wands made from driftwood and decorated with magical symbols using pyrography if we don't have the aptitude with a knife. Miniature wands can be extremely useful as magical batteries for any impromptu working you may have to carry out when away from the seashore. They are small and unobtrusive and can be tucked away in a bag or pocket. Use driftwood that has already been cleansed and empowered by the sea, but do keep all magical items separate from each other, or they can lose much of their magical properties.

Glass fishing floats are now popular collectors' items. They were once used by fishermen in many parts of the world to keep their nets afloat. Large groups of fishnets strung together, sometimes 50 miles long, were set adrift in the ocean and supported near the surface by hollow glass balls to give them buoyancy. The earliest evidence of glass floats being used by fishermen comes from Norway in 1844, where small egg-sized floats were used with fishing line and hooks. Japan started using the glass floats as early as 1910.

Most of the remaining floats originated in Japan because it had a large, deep-sea fishing industry. These glass floats are no longer being used by fishermen, but many of them are still afloat in the world's oceans, primarily the Pacific. The author has a dark blue Japanes float that was washed up on the California shore and sent via surface mail to England – crossing two oceans on its journey. These have become popular collectors' item for beachcombers and decorators, although replicas are also being manufactured. Genuine floats can be found in antique shops, often still wrapped in their nets and today have found other uses.

- As 'witch-balls' to be hung by the entrance to the sea-witch's home for protection against negative influences entering the house: suspended from the ceiling in the original net to 'absorb' any malign energies that are captured by the reflective surface.

- Or used for skrying: dark blue, dark green or deep red glass balls making the best tools. The glass floats are utilised in exactly the same way as a traditional witch's crystal ball ... and if the float has a genuine history of being washed by the sea (rather than a replica), it can produce some amazing results.

It's not just being out at sea where danger can threaten, we also have to remind ourselves of the immense power the sea has over the land. In classical mythology, the Greeks referred to Poseidon, god of the sea as the 'Earth Shaker' and if we stand on the shore during the time of the winter storms, it soon becomes evident that the waves – which consist of tons of water, hurled violently and almost incessantly against the shore – do far more than merely level the sand and discolour the rocks.

Foaming waves thunder across the beaches and leap against the cliffs, sea-walls and piers; having the power to wrench apart the massive blocks of an esplanade … 'They assault the cliffs not merely with their own impetus but with boulders like battering-rams, pebbles like projectiles, and masses of sand like an abrasive powder.' Not surprising that both the Greek and Roman sea-gods, Poiseidon and Neptune, are associated with the power of the horse …the speed of the incoming tide often being compared to being 'faster than galloping horses'.

When they strike the shore, the waves drive the air before them, compressing it against the cliff face; when released it expands violently with almost an explosive effect, weakening and ripping away part of the cliff. As we have seen in an earlier chapter, this compressed air is even more destructive when it is forced into the rock crevices and left free to expand. In this way, the waves destroy the cliffs, undermining them until the upper part collapses.

Nowhere is the power and mystery of the sea more apparent than in the magical world of the sea-cave. We know that the power of the sea has the strength to transform the landscape in a constantly battle of the elements, but the world of the sea-cave is one of silence. The quiet is broken only by the drip of water; and the plain surface of the rock 'decorated' with strange colouring where minerals have stained the walls. This underground world provided the earliest known dwellings for Neanderthal man just prior to the last Ice Age. In more 'modern' times, caves offered privacy to those of traditional Craft during the years of persecution, and have always been the favourite meeting place for witches.

Pathworking to the sea cave

The solitary Vigil is an integral part of every witch's learning and for those who have access to a sea-cave with an entrance protected by deep water, this is the ideal spot for this to take place. Do remember, however, that if the tide is running high, you risk the danger of becoming trapped – and even drowned.

Many years ago, a friend was due to undergo his Vigil in such a cave and at the appointed hour he was rowed into the cave and left alone in the darkness on a dry rocky platform to complete his solitary 'watch'. For sometime after the splashing of the oars had died away, he relaxed into the silence, wrapped up in his sleeping-bag. Then, out of the darkness came a slithering sound accompanied by heavy breathing. With the hair standing up on the back of his neck, he listened to the noise coming nearer, until a sudden pressure against his leg almost frightened him out of his wits.

Unable to bear the situation any longer, he turned on the emergency torch and found himself staring into the eyes of a young seal! No doubt the animal thought the figure trussed up in a sleeping-bag was a member of the family, but for the 'watcher' it was a truly magical moment. He'd entered the world of a wild animal and for a few hours been accepted in trust; the seal revealed itself as his 'totem' animal from that time on. Some hours later, the creature slipped back into the water, and moments later he caught the sound of oars in the water … his Vigil was over.

Using this imagery, try your own pathworking to the sea-cave

Make yourself comfortable in a place where you will not be disturbed and, casting your circle of protection, prepare for a unique spiritual experience.

It is dusk. Begin by stepping into the prow of a boat in the company of cowled oarsmen who will row you across the deep waters that guard the entrance to the cave. As you pass into the shadow of the overhanging cliffs, a lantern is lit and far ahead, the light catches the ripples on the surface of the black water. There is darkness all around now, the lantern casting eerie shadows on the ceiling of the cavern, but outside the ring of light, there is only an inky stillness.

Soon the prow scrapes against rock and the company has reached the inner cavern with its dry, sand-covered floor, deep inside the towering cliff. You step out of the boat and, without a word, the oarsmen row back the way they came ... in the dying glow from the lantern, you just have time to glimpse the cathedral-like rock formations of the vast cavern. Here you will spend the night ... in the darkness ... deep in the earth ... protected by a barrier of water ... alone.

Moving away from the water's edge, your feet sink into the soft sand but you need to climb higher into the cavern to begin your Watch. The place is dark and silent but you draw your cloak around yourself and settle down for the duration of the night. Even in this vaulted silence there is sound ... the constant drip of water and the steady beating of your heart ... it has slowed down after the first adrenalin rush of finding yourself in this strange environment.

Concentrate on the pulsating rhythm and use it as the beat of an inner drum, lulling you into a trance state; ready to receive whatever images and visions the pathworking is likely to bring. This is your very own moment where you commune with the sea and the Earth ...deep inside an astral cavern that has been created by the ceaseless pounding of the waves ...

When you come out of the pathworking, clap your hands to disperse the astral 'bubble' and earth yourself. Make sure that you have some biscuits and a hot drink to hand. You may have spent only moments on another plane ... or it may have been hours ... but your body will be reacting to the 'astral cold' of the cavern, and the hot drink will serve to both 'earth' and warm you. Reflect on the journey you have just made, and record the results in your magical journal.

Danger zones

Having encountered the astral 'sea cave', we must also realise that even the most harmless coastlines are fraught with hidden dangers. In understanding what these dangers are, however, means that a) it reduces our fear of the 'unknown' and, b) affords us another working 'tool'. For the sea-witch, these *natural* dangers represent the mirrored dangers we may encounter on the astral: dangers that can engulf us if we don't keep our minds on the work in hand.

Quicksands

Quicksands are deposited by the tide as its flow slackens, or scooped up from a shallow seafloor by the waves; an offshore sand bar (as dangerous as a reef in bad weather, consisting of very fine sand or silt, saturated with water and rendered slimy by clay) forms a deadly quicksand. They are known to occur where an abnormal amount of water is trapped in the ground by a layer of clay and are found anywhere water and sand mix every day: such as ocean coasts, near sandy creeks, and can be from only a few inches to several feet deep. A beach may have quicksands one year and not the next; occasionally they are caused by springs on beaches with steep sides.

Quicksand will hold you fast and the more you thrash about, the deeper you will sink – and eventually drown if the tide is coming in. This is where the sea-witch's staff comes into its own. It *is* possible to float in quicksand, just as you would in the sea, providing you move slowly and allow the sandy liquid to flow under your body. If your staff doesn't reach the bottom of the pocket to reassure you that the patch is shallow, lay the staff on the quicksand and pull yourself over it until it rests beneath your back. Use the staff for leverage to raise your legs onto firmer ground.

From a magical perspective

If our magical learning isn't built on firm foundations, sooner or later we will find ourselves slipping further and further into the mire, because we don't have the knowledge to cope with the false image we've created for ourselves. There's many a witch whose built up a bogus reputation for themselves, only to flounder in the quicksands of exposure, when their carefully created self-image fails to stand up under the scrutiny of those with a genuine magical training.

The staff is a magical tool that can be carried in public without causing comment — but it can also save our lives if we suddenly have to turn to the magical power stored *within* it. One of the most important magical lessons is: Know Thyself and by developing an understanding of where the magical quicksands may be waiting to trap the unsuspecting, we lessen the risk of allowing our enthusiasm to out-pace our abilities.

Fog

As any sailor will tell you, they much prefer to be caught out in strong winds at sea, than a thick fog. Even on the beach or coastal path, fog can have a disorienting effect, which is equally as dangerous. Fog, mist and cloud are all formed when air cools to 'dew point' ... at ground level, the 'cloud' is called fog or mist depending upon the visibility. At sea, this is defined as fog when visibility is 1000 yards or less; mist is a visibility between 1–2000 yards. [On land, fog is used when visibility is 220 yards or less.]

When warm and moist air flows from an area of warm sea to colder waters, this produces a sea-fog, which can occur at any time of the day, even with quite strong winds about. With winds over F4–5 (see Chapter Five), the result may be low cloud and poor visibility rather than fog. Around the east coast of Britain, sea-fog is always possible when the wind is in the east because the sea temperatures in the middle of the North Sea are always warmer than those waters near the coast. This creates the persistent 'sea-fret' that causes a miserable overcast day near the coast, while inland it is warm and sunny.

In the English Channel, sea-fog can occur at any time of the year, but seems to be more common in the late spring and early to mid-summer, when the water inshore is still fairly cold. Fog is more frequent in July than January, because stronger winds in January will usually lift the fog into low cloud. Around the Channel Islands, sea-fog may be more likely in late spring with a westerly wind; later in the year, however, it will also occur with an easterly wind. The water near the French coast gets warm in the summer, while the water around the islands stays comparatively cold.

Writing about fog, sailor Frank Singleton, added this one: 'Not normally mention in the books is what I call thunderstorm-fog. This can follow those thundery outbreaks that drift slowly up from Spain and France.' Although the thunderstorms may have ceased, there can be a great deal of very damp air around and this all too easily can be cooled by the cold waters, say, near the Channel Islands, to give a very dense and persistent fog. Being lost in the fog is an eerie and unnerving experience, whether at sea or ashore. All sense of direction is lost and, as another sailor friend says: 'It's better to avoid fog than have to deal with it.'

[NB: Haze is the reduction of visibility due to smoke or dust in the air.]

From a magical perspective

Magically speaking, fog is our own 'veil of illusion' in which sound, vision and senses become distorted and we lose our way. Fog or sea-mist corresponds to the Moon card in the Tarot: Here we find ... 'a weird, deceptive life. The knight upon this quest has to rely on the three lower senses: touch, taste and smell. Such light as there may be is deadlier than darkness ... This is the threshold of life; this is the threshold of death. All is doubtful; all is mysterious; all is intoxicating.'

It can, however, also provide us with a natural 'cloak of invisibility', in that we can conduct our magical workings concealed by a blanket of sea-mist. The choice is ours. If we chose to tread a magical pathway, groping blindly through the fog, then sooner or later we will become totally lost and disorientated. Or we use the concealing mist to our advantage and embrace the adventure, knowing we have a firm grounding in magical technique.

Empowering the guardian
In Chapter Three we talked about finding a skull at the water margin. Mostly these will have belonged to fish or birds but occasionally the remains of an animal might be washed up on the shore. If we feel that we can work with the bones of a dead creature, this will provide us with an extremely powerfully protective amulet in the form of a spirit guardian.

Here we are looking at – for want of a better explanation – the shamanic technique of creating a 'spirit house' for working on the inner levels where death and life become one and the same. The rest of the corpse should be buried with appropriate rites to set the soul of the animal free and the skull taken home. This can be cleansed by burying it in sand and salt for several months, or by soaking it in a bleach/water solution to remove any remaining flesh.

From a magical perspective
When the 'spirit house' has been thoroughly cleansed, prepare the rite by casting the Circle. Place the skull on the altar with a single candle burning behind it. Prick your finger and use the blood to trace your personal sigil on the bone between the eyes of

the skull. Now place your hands on either side of the skull and channel your witch-power to flow between them. As the energy builds, place your two middle fingers into the eye sockets. You have now created a powerful spirit pathway and may even feel a mild electric shock.

Focus on the space behind the sigil, i.e. where's the creature's brain would have been, and allow the visions to manifest. Close your eyes and follow the creature's natural path … a bird in flight, a fish swimming in the ocean, an animal in its natural habitat … the path is now yours to follow.

Needless to say, this 'spirit house' *must* be kept away from prying eyes and inquisitive fingers. It is also necessary to make provision for its disposal at your death, or the spirit will remain earthbound and restless if it is not given its release. There are several instructions that can be given to a trusted friend. One is that the skull be buried (or cremated) with you, or that it be taken away and buried with appropriate rites near the place where it was originally found. Secondly, that no one should attempt to take over the 'spirit house' as their own.

Sadly, too many witches and magicians fail to make provision for their magical tools and equipment, and often these will be sold off as curios without being 'magically de-commissioned'. A sealed codicil left for the executors should contain a detailed list of what should happen to *all* magical possessions and books, and in particular relate to those personal items that will need to be disposed of sympathetically. This would generally include any personal papers, magical journals, the witch's robe and cord, the knife (unless this has been specifically willed to someone), any symbolic jewellery and altar equipment and, of course, any 'spirit houses' and familiars, both of which need to be released by an experienced magical practitioner.

Celestial navigation

Although the sea-witch may never leave the land, it is important to realise that 'celestial' or astro-navigation plays an important part in the seafarer's life. If any heavenly body and the horizon can be seen anywhere in the world, a position line can be established within 10–15 minutes. Accuracy to within 10 miles is possible under rough conditions, and to within 2 miles under moderate to favourable conditions. By day, the sun and often the moon can be used; the moon and planets can be used at twilight, and under favourable conditions, the stars can be used in darkness.

From a magical perspective

Observing the stars also has a magical quality, in that we have a ready-made map of the seasons and, generally speaking, one that is not affected by light pollution as it is inland.

Here we can sit back and watch the easily identifiable circum-polar stars in Ursa Major and Minor, Draco, and Cassiopeia as they circle around the Pole Star (Polaris) because while the Earth spins around its own axis, it is also tracing out a path around the Sun. These two motions, and where we are standing on Earth, determine what we see in the sky at any given time. As we move through the seasons, these giant constellations change their positions, sometimes appearing to dip down towards the horizon; at other times they are directly overhead.

Other constellations, such as Orion 'disappear' in the spring to re-merge again in the autumn, while Pegasus and the Summer Triangle follow their own paths through the heavens. The movement of the stars gives the sea-witch a truly magical calendar with which to work, and it pays to make a study of the main constellations in order to 'read' the signs in the heavens: and not just in terms of zodiacal astrology.

There no escape ...

The importance of understanding the natural tides was discussed earlier in the book, and we return to the subject again towards the end, hoping the message has gone home. Yes, it *will* mean jettisoning all the pre-conditioning about set dates in the calendar but if we are going to work as a sea-witch, we are only interested in the natural tides.

We know that the moon circles the earth once every 27.3 days, rotating to keep the same face turned towards the Earth. The Earth, however, shows all its faces to the moon once every 24.8 hours. This means that the waters of the Earth flow out toward the moon, bringing high tide to any land that lies in that direction. Every drop of water in the ocean responds to this force, and every living marine animal and plant responds to the rhythm ...

'But what if I don't live near the sea?' you may interrupt.

It doesn't matter, because there's no escaping the pull of the natural tides, even inland. **Remember the story of the oysters?**

Dr Lyall Watson recorded his explanation in his book *Supernature*, when he cited the experiments of a colleague, 'an indefatigable researcher into natural rhythms' who lived and worked a thousand miles from the sea. For obvious reasons, most marine research centres are established on the coast, and in laboratory experiments, researchers found that oysters had a marked tidal rhythm. They opened their shells to feed at high tide and closed them to prevent damage and drying out during the ebb.

In laboratory tanks they kept this rhythm going, so one member of the team decided to take some home to Illinois to monitor them more closely. His home was inland, on the shore of Lake Michigan but even there the oysters continued to remember the tidal rhythm of their home on Long Island Sound. This continued for two weeks, but on the fifteenth day a slippage in the rhythm had occurred. The oysters were no longer opening and closing in harmony with the tide that washed their native shore, and it appeared as if the experiment had gone wrong. In fact the all the oysters' behaviour had altered in the same way and they were still keeping time with each other.

The researcher calculated the difference between the old

rhythm and the new, and discovered that the oysters now opened up at the time the tide would have flooded locally – had his home been on the coast and not perched on the bank of one of the Great Lakes, some 580 feet above sea level. The oysters had been able to recalculate their tidal time-table and serve as a reminder that the same gravitational force of the moon that acts on the ocean can also act on very much smaller bodies of water inland. The researcher studied his oysters' new rhythm with the movement of the moon and found that most of them were opening when the moon was directly overhead.

From a magical perspective

When most us began to learn about 'magic', we soaked up the occult propaganda about the annual celebrations falling on specific dates in the calendar, and this information has been subsequently recorded in hundreds of magical journals and *Books of Shadows* for generations of new witches. It is not until we work with the *natural* tides that we realise these so-called 'Great Sabbats' are no longer synchronised to coincide with the Earth and its natural rhythms. The periodic 'massaging' of the calendar has meant that the official dates for these celebrations have been moved around quite a bit since they were first incorporated into the Church calendar. But on the coast there is no escaping from the natural tides as everyone's life is completely bound by them.

Whilst we will all agree that group-dynamics can raise power for magical working, so that even the most ineffectual member of the coven can contribute. For the solitary sea-witch, working with natural tides can compensate for the lack of input by other parties. Group energy keeps everyone on track, but it all needs synchronising within the Circle in order for the working to be successful. The solitary sea-witch merely 'plugs-in' to whatever is going on around her (or him), at any time and place.

If we work alone and are drawn to the sheer magnitude of

oceanic power, then we forget about the 'how-to' books, and work direct with the forces of natural energy that are there for the asking on a *daily* basis.

The Sea Witch's curse

Not that we would suggest for one moment that sea-witches go around placing curses on folk, but no book on Craft would be complete without a suitable 'hex'. As far as we can tell, this rather unpleasant one has its origins in southern France, and we've seen similar variations attributed to other parts of Europe so, as the saying goes, 'you takes your pick, and takes your chance'.

Cursing, or ill-wishing, isn't confined to witches but when dealing with magic, it is always advisable to have one or two tricks up your sleeve, as other folk may not be so reticent about demonstrating their magical prowess. Curses, once thrown, cannot be undone, they can only be deflected; so it is advisable for anyone tempted to play about with this kind of magical operation to understand the repercussions. This version leaves no doubt as to the outcome, which condemns the victim to becoming entangled in the seaweed and pulled down into the depths of the ocean ...

Go down, go down, my pretty youth,
But you will not come up
Tangled mind will twist and turn
And tangled foot will follow.
You will go down, my pretty one,
But you will not come up again.
So tangle, tangle, twist and turn,
For tangling webs are woven.

Hopefully, the horrible implications of this curse would dissuade anyone from throwing it, especially as curses have a habit of rebounding on the sender. The dark side of the sea is scary enough!

Fruits de mer

The 'fruits of the sea' is the name applied to crustaceans and shellfish of various kinds, which are served together, raw or cooked. In addition to the more familiar lobsters, crabs, scallops, clams, mussels, oysters and cockles, there are other foods to be harvested from the sea.

Sea anemones:
Or *anémones de mer* is the name commonly given to actinia or starfish, the edible molluscs that abound on the coasts of France, particularly on the Mediterranean side.

Sea kale:
Or *chou marin*, to give it its culinary name, grows wild on the coast of most of western Europe. It takes the form of a strong root out of which grow leaf rosettes consisting of long thick stalks terminating in fringed, rounded crests. These so-called leaves are pale in colour, almost white. Seakale is eaten in the same way as asparagus and has a nutty flavour.

Sea urchin:
Or *oursin* is the popular name given to the marine animals of the echinus species, several of which are edible. The most delicate are to be found around the coasts of Japan and in the Mediterranean.

Rock samphire:
Crithmum maritimum flowers in June-August in cliffs and rocks. Collectors of gulls' eggs used to pick rock samphire during May and send it to London in barrels of sea-water. It has a distinctive scent and was used for making sauces and pickles.

Sea wrack:

Also known as rock-weed and *fucus*, is a species of seaweed that has been used as a food supplement in times of scarcity in the northern hemisphere. In Scotland the young stems of the tangle or sea-lettuce are sometimes eaten as a salad. In the Far East, however, seaweed is part of the staple diet. Seaweed grows throughout the world and edible varieties are eaten in varying quantities in Japan, China, Iceland, Britain, Scandinavia and North America.

Laver:

Porphyra umbilicalis is found around the coasts of Britain and other temperate countries bordering on the Pacific and Atlantic coasts. Laver is widely used in Japan in salads, soups, biscuits, stews, preserves and sweetmeats. In terms of traditional food, however, the most famous must be the *lawr* or laverbread of Wales. Laver (*porphyra laciniata*) and green laver (*ulva latissima*) are the same as *sloke* in Ireland and Scotland, but they are in much greater daily use in South Wales, particularly in the Swansea and south Pembroke-shire areas. Laver is a smooth, fine seaweed, sometimes called sea-spinach, which clings to the rocks like silk.

At one time it was cured in drying houses, but nowadays more technical methods are used to process it. It is sold in markets and many other places already prepared, when it resembles a dark brownish, spinach-like gelatine purée, ready for use. *Bara lawr* –or laverbread – is a misleading name for it does not resemble bread at all, but the puree described above. Mix prepared laverbread with a good sprinkling of fine oatmeal, then shape into little cakes and fry in bacon fat; or coat the laverbread in oatmeal, fry in fat and serve with grilled ham or bacon, sprinkled with a little onion juice or lemon.

Wales is also famous for its cockles and for centuries,

the vast cockle beds of Pen-clawdd stretched out into the Burry Estuary. Here, the cockle-women rode out on ponies or donkeys to gather their harvest, which lie a few inches below the muddy sand, the cockles being scooped up and carried in wicker baskets. Traditionally, local cockles are served in pies and soups, or simply plain boiled, shelled and served with brown bread and butter, with a dash of vinegar or lemon. Cockles are from the same family as clams and there are over two hundred varieties. Much of the Welsh crop is exported to the continent and news of the 'cockle wars' still feature in the local newspapers.

Magical tasks and exercises

As we have seen, living and working by the seashore offers a different perspective on the natural tides and energies for the sea-witch and by now it will be obvious why many of the seasonal rites of the inland witch would be inappropriate here, where sea and land collide.

We are also conscious that the times and tides that govern a southern or western coast, will differ considerably from a sea-witch working on northern or eastern shores. This is why it is important to create our own personal Magical Diary and begin to formulate your own seasonal workings and observations.

If you haven't already got one, buy a suitable book in which to record the phases of the moon for the coming year.

Paying special attention to the new and full moons, record the times of the daily high tides.

The dark of the moon — or the 'slack tide' should also be recorded because this generates a different kind of energy, and many witches find they get good results at this time.

Using the solstices and the equinoxes plan your own sea-calendar in order to celebrate the changing face of the seashore.

Record a special date of your own to observe every year (i.e. some anniversary of a dedication, perhaps), and try to observe this in your own way.

Celebratory Rite (Indoors)

An indoor rite is best celebrated in the form of a 'feast' and what better way than to serve a sea-food supper, accompanied by plenty of fresh, crusty bread, salad and chilled white wine. Or if the weather is cold and miserable, what's wrong with a really good 'fish supper'?

This should be looked upon as a gathering of friends and may not necessarily be a witches-only affair, so the rite takes on the form of a normal supper-party. The blessing of the food or the Invocation can be made before the guests arrive and a portion set to one side for the offering without anyone being any the wiser.

Create the atmosphere as you would normally for a rite, with candle-light and appropriate music ... but go easy on the incense as this could jar unpleasantly with the smell of food.

Remember that these rites are a throw-back to the times when the fishing fleet provided a livelihood for the whole community and this celebration would be the equivalent of an inland harvest-home. It is not a time for asking for anything but a time for thanking the powers-that-be for their bounty during the summer months, or their protection in seeing you through the deprivations of the winter months.

Note: Unfortunately, a lot of people are allergic to shell-fish, so do make sure that you are familiar with any problems this may cause for any of your guests. Shell-fish poisoning can be extremely dangerous.

Chapter Seven

Toward the Sea

As we now realise, the sea covers well over half of the earth's surface and at its deepest goes down over 30,000 feet through that vast underwater landscape of plateaux, ridges, plains, bottomless trenches, mountain ranges and rugged rock pillars, whose volcanic caps form the oceanic islands. If we look at a map of the ocean's floor, however, we are confronted by an alien vista that would seem more appropriate to some gloomy planet on the far side of the galaxy than anywhere here on Earth. This cold, grey, submarine environment is remote, inhospitable and frightening in its strangeness.

Nevertheless, there comes a time in everyone's magical life when we feel the need to push our personal boundaries, and working with the power of the Deep is no exception. But why does this siren's song, this powerful lure of the sea, have a stronger hold over some, and not others? Professor Barry Cunliffe opens his deceptively mystical book, *Facing the Ocean*, with this highly evocative visualisation, and encapsulates in a single paragraph how our distant ancestors looked upon the sea and how it shaped their lives ...

To stand on a sea-washed promontory looking westwards at sunset over the Atlantic is to share a timeless human experience. We are in awe of the unchanging and unchangeable as all have been before us and all will be. Wonder is tempered with reassurance: it is an end, but we are content in the knowledge that the cycle will reproduce itself – the sun will reappear. The sea below creates different, more conflicting emotions. True, there is the comforting inevitability of the tides, but there is also an unpredictability of mood, the sea constantly changing, sometimes erupting in crescendos of brute force destroying and remoulding the land and claiming human life. The sea is a balance of opposites. It gives and takes. It can destroy land and quickly build new; it sustains life and it can kill. Small wonder that through time communities have sought to explain these forces in terms of myth and have attempted to gain some puny influence over them through propitiation ...

According to Cunliffe, 10,000 years of history reveals a kinship amongst the ancient peoples of the Atlantic seaboard, whose lands faced the turbulent ocean and whose rich cultures and identities reflect that shared experience. As we would expect with what was then an oral tradition of story-telling, many of the regional folk-tales differ in detail, but the basic story remains constant. Professor Cunliffe suggests that these may have been actual events that passed into folk-memory, and spread along the Atlantic seaways; or that they were part of a much older myth, common to the Atlantic coasts, which helped to explain the 'unstable equilibrium between land and sea'.

And, as if to endorse this idea, echoes of all these ancient folk-myths are still to be found in the rich sea-lore, superstition and belief all around the Atlantic coastlines; many of those superstitions travelling across the ocean with our maritime ancestors.

In those early days, however, the ocean, was viewed as being 'limitless and impassable'. Emerging biblical traditions held it to be a place of darkness and power, from which would emerge the apocalyptic beast that would destroy mankind and herald the end of the world.

As we come to realise, our psychic connection with the sea is no illusion, but a historical reality from which we subconsciously draw on ancestral memories, no matter where we live on the planet. And like all areas of magic, we need to explore that history in order to gain the **knowledge** as a key to the **wisdom** of the ancients. Only then can we hope to reach any form of **understanding**.

Universal subconsciousness

Much of the archetypical sea-myth that forms a large part of what magical practitioners recognise as the 'universal subconscious', was formulated from early tales told by returning sailors, of fearsome monsters and fabulous islands located far out in the western ocean. These early adventures 'soon became enmeshed in a web of fantasy to emerge into literature as the *immrama* (tales of voyages) ...the allegorical content, rich in metaphor and symbolic meaning', touching the very souls of the listeners ... who believed in the existence of these islands, many of which even appeared on sea-maps of the time. In other words, metaphor and reality had merged into each other.

From these obscure origins, tales would have been further embellished and embroidered to explain the strange phenomena linked to the sea. For example, the remnants of submerged forests, only visible at very low tide, provided graphic evidence of drowned landscapes. Even more disconcerting to the superstitious medieval mind would have been the sight of the blackened roots of old oak trees thrusting up through the sands. It wasn't difficult for a fertile imagination to visualise images of drowned villages and divine retribution, when what they were really looking at were the remains of Early Bronze Age forests, slowly submerging over a span of centuries by a gradually rising sea-level.

Nevertheless, the widely travelled Strabo, writing in his 17-volume *Geographica*, says: 'All discussion respecting the gods requires an examination of ancient opinions, and of fables, since the ancients expressed enigmatically their physical notions concerning the nature of things, and always intermixed fable with their discoveries.' In other words, even from classical times we were being warned against taking things too literally when it comes to the interpretation of myth and magical lore.

And yet, published archaeological evidence reveals that the distribution pattern of Bronze Age artefacts in the west of Britain and the Continent was a result of transport by sea. As the pattern of these artefacts came more fully to be understood, so the importance of the Atlantic seaways began to be appreciated by pre-historians. There is even the suggestion that the distribution of megalithic tombs in western Europe are a result of 'megalithic missionaries' sailing along the coast, taking with them the belief system that required community effort to build the great monuments.

So the sea (or our 'ancestral connections' with the sea) is a vital part of a sea-witch's heritage – it is in our blood, our unconscious memory, and our ultimate safe haven.

Isles of the Blessed

In the Isles of the Blessed, heroes and other favored mortals in Greek and Celtic mythology were received by the gods into a blissful paradise. These islands were thought to lie in the Western Ocean near the encircling River Oceanus: Madeira, the Canary Islands, and Cape Verde have sometimes been cited as possible matches. It was the Greek poet Hesiod, who first wrote of those who 'untroubled in spirit dwell in islands of the blest by deep-eddying Ocean, happy heroes for whom the grain-giving fields bear rich honey-sweet fruit three times a year'.

It's been suggested that this was little more than a 'comforting metaphor' to help people come to terms with the inevitability of death, in much the same way as later religions created their own concepts of heaven or paradise. Nevertheless, it is easy to understand why the earliest beliefs placed the Islands beyond the ocean, in the direction of the setting sun, and why the image remained a powerful theme well into the Middle Ages, and up to the present day.

The first British concept appears in Geoffrey of Monmouth's 1136 pseudo-historical account *Historia Regum Britanniae* (*The History of the Kings of Britain*). He dealt with the subject in more detail in *Vita Merlini*, in which he describes for the first time in Arthurian legend, the enchantress Morgan le Fay as the chief of nine sisters who live on the island of Avalon, and his description of the island indicates that a sea voyage was needed to get there. His description also reveals the magical nature of the island:

The island of apples which men call 'The Fortunate Isle' gets its name from the fact that it produces all things of itself; the fields there have no need of the ploughs of the farmers and all cultivation is lacking except what nature provides. Of its own accord it produces grain and grapes, and apple trees grow in its woods from the close-clipped grass. The ground of it own accord produces everything instead of merely grass ...

Referred to as 'Insula Avallonis' in the *Histori*, in the later *Vita Merlini* Geoffrey called it 'Insula Pomorum' – the isle of apples. It seems most likely that the word is of Celtic origin; the word for 'apple' in modern Welsh is *afal*, and *aval* being 'apple' in modern Cornish. As an 'Isle of the Blessed' Avalon also has parallels in many Indo-European mythologies, in particular the Irish Tír na nÓg, and the Greek Hesperides, also noted for its apples. J R R Tolkien later used the concept of 'going into the West' in *The Lord of the Rings* as the final destination of the Elves when they leave the world of men.

It's an over-used analogy to say that life is a journey, but it is an accurate description of how we are all swept along to an inevitable end. Our journey begins in the misty and mysterious fountain that wells up amongst the rocks on the distant mountain slopes of childhood. It passes through the changing scenery of swift flowing brooks and streams of adolescence, often becoming confused in murky backwaters, swamps and marshes before entering the calmer tributaries and rivulets of adulthood. The vast river moves through our mature years until we reach the estuary and shore of the great sea where this journey ends – and another begins.

The spectre of Death and the sea are never far removed from

each other. For the sea-witch there is an obligation to honour our departed ancestors (whether we believe them to be over the sea, or under it), which is not out of place with the observations traditionally carried out at Samhain. In all aspects of traditional Craft there are strong associations with Otherworld and a powerful element of ancestor-worship – for the sea-witch there is no difference.

In nautical terms, 'to be sent to Davy Jones's Locker' is used as a euphemism for death at sea or, more precisely, the resting place of drowned sailors, The name 'Davy Jones' being a nickname for what would be the malevolent spirit of the sea, and although the origins of the name are unclear, this nautical superstition was only popularized in the 1800s. The earliest known reference to the negative connotation of Davy Jones occurs in Tobias Smollett's *The Adventures of Peregrine Pickle*, published in 1751:

This same Davy Jones, according to sailors, is the fiend that presides over all the evil spirits of the deep, and is often seen   in various shapes, perching among the rigging on the eve of hurricanes: shipwrecks, and other disasters to which sea-faring life is exposed, warning the devoted wretch of death and woe.

In traditional Craft, too, there is no boundary in the relationship between the living and the dead. The sea-witch reveres those who have lived on and died at sea, even if there are no ties of blood. In death they become 'the ancestors', a collective energy that is as old as mankind, and constantly augmented with every 'crossing the bar'.

Sunset and evening star
And one clear call for me!
And may there be no moaning at the bar,
When I put out to sea ...
        [*Crossing the Bar* – Tennyson]

It is therefore important that a day be set aside each year (possibly around the time of Samhain or All Hallows), during which to offer some form of propitiation at the water's edge. The object of this rite is to ensure the ancestors' continued well-being and positive disposition towards the living – and sometimes to ask for special favours or assistance. This ancestral belief requires us to have faith in an afterlife, and in a survival (at least for a time) of a personal identity beyond death. This concept is not just confined to traditional witchcraft and rather than being thought unusual, it remains an important component of various religious practices in modern times.

The non-religious function of this form of ancestor veneration is to cultivate kinship values like clan loyalty, and continuity of the tradition's lineage. The more the sea-witch is aware of these Otherworldly currents that carry us through life, the better we can steer our course. For the sea-witch, the sea is a symbol of death ... or rather the end of this life and the beginning of the next.

We must be still and still moving
Into another intensity
For a further union, a deeper communion
Through the dark cold and the empty desolation,
The wave cry, the wind cry, the vast waters
Of the petrel and the porpoise. In the end is my beginning.
[T S Eliot – *East Coker II*]

'So mote it be!'

Mysteries of the Deep

As we know, the sea floor lies at depths ranging from zero to more than 36,000 feet below the surface of the ocean. In many places, this surface is a flat monotonous expanse – the abyssal plains. Elsewhere, it has been shaped by a combination of tectonic and volcanic activity to form the features of its massive mountain ranges, deep trenches and basins.

However, located on the mid-ocean ridges, at an average depth of about 7,000 feet are some spectacular features called hydrothermal vents. These vents are like hot springs continuously spewing out copious amounts of scalding mineral-rich seawater. Some of these vents solidified into tall chimneys and when the super-heated water contacts the near-freezing seawater, the minerals form particles that add to the height of the stacks. Some of these chimney structures can reach heights of nearly 200 feet. An example of such a towering vent was 'Godzilla', a structure in the Pacific Ocean near Oregon that reached 130 feet high before it fell over.

The chimnies that emit clouds of black material are called 'black smokers', named for the dark hue of the particles. These formations support a diverse community of primitive life-forms; and are among the most extreme environments on the planet in which *living* organisms can survive. 'White smokers' are vents that emit lighter-hued minerals, such as those containing barium, calcium, and silicon. These vents also tend to have lower temperature plumes. The areas around hydrothermal vents host complex communities of diverse organisms, including giant tube worms, clams, limpets and shrimp despite the water emerging from a vent reaching temperatures ranging up to 400°C, compared to a typical 2°C for the surrounding deep ocean!

Life has traditionally been seen as driven by energy from the sun, but deep sea organisms have no access to sunlight, so they must depend on nutrients found in the dusty chemical deposits and hydrothermal fluids in which they live. This eco-system is reliant upon the continued existence of the 'hydrothermal vent field as the primary source of energy', which differs from most surface life on Earth which is based on solar energy.

Visualisation: The descent to the deep ocean floor on a research submarine usually lasts about two hours – the time taken to fall with a spiralling motion through more than a mile of sea water. The crew can travel through the strange landscape and observe the sea floor, lit by the submarine's powerful lights, through remote video cameras and small windows. In 1979, scientists in *Alvin* dove to the Mid-Ocean Ridge in the eastern Pacific. A spectacular sight greeted them. Clouds of what looked like black smoke were billowing from tall chimneys on the ocean floor.

This stunning discovery on the bottom of the Pacific Ocean changed our understanding of planet Earth and life on it. They found a superheated plume of muddy water was pouring out of the sea floor: gushing shimmering, warm, mineral-rich fluids into the cold, dark depths. And, to their complete surprise, they found that the vents were brimming with extraordinary, unexpected life.

These discoveries have opened up a tantalising possibility. Not only are the mid-ocean ridges the birthplace of the oceanic crust that covers most of the Earth's surface ... but they may be the birthplace of life itself! Genetic studies suggest that these organisms are off-shoots from the lowest branches of the tree of life, and their primordial nature is also suggested by the fact that the oldest-known fossils are also the remains of single-celled organisms that thrived near hot springs about 3.5 million years ago. The ocean floor, far from being ancient and dead, has proved to be one of the most dynamic and mysterious places on Earth.

So ... sit comfortably in chair in a darkened room, surrounded by a protective Circle; if possible, utilise a faint blue or green digital light from something electrical that will simulate the interior light of a submarine. Sit for a while in the quiet and try to clear your mind of all mundane things. You are encapsulated in a tiny space ... now ... using the mind-pictures described above, visualise looking out through the tiny porthole and into the cone of light illuminating the seabed. You are looking upon a scene similar to that took place when Life was first emerging from the primordial waters.

Confined in the tiny space of the capsule, you are an observer of this emerging life, the reality rendered inaccessible by thousands of tons of water pressure and, outside the cone of light, a cold, inky darkness. Unlike the thunderous sequences of Stravinsky's *Rite of Spring* as shown in the film, *Fantasia*, this is a silent birthplace. Using your imagination, project your thoughts out into the underwater seascape in front of you, and see what images come to you from the Deep.

You cannot stay long in this place of silence, where the tiny submarine has become for the moment, your astral temple. Soon the vessel rises to the surface and you slowly return to the mundane world. Allow yourself several minutes to come out of your visualisation and to completely dispel any remnants of astral energy, clap your hands loudly. Take a hot drink and sweet biscuit to complete the 'earthing' process.

This visualisation exercise enables us to descend into the Deep as a casual *observer*, which means we retain control over our actions. For pathworking, we follow the same basic preliminaries of setting the scene in our imagination, but this time we are diving without a safety line. Instead of retaining complete control over our 'dive', at a certain point we become a *partic-ipant*, allowing ourselves to be taken over by the astral currents and surrendering to an altered state of consciousness.

During the visualisation technique there was also the security of knowing the hull of the 'astral submarine' would act as a barrier between ourselves and anything unpleasant or threat-ening. For this descent into the Abyss, our lifeline is a tiny pinprick of blue light shimmering in the distance, like a candle viewed from the wrong end of a telescope. Should at any time we feel afraid, we only have to head for this blue light and we will emerge from the pathworking without let or hindrance.

Pathworking: into the abyss

We've learn that water has a slightly bluish tint, which intercepts the reds and yellows of daylight much more quickly than the other colours, so that only the blues and greens can penetrate to any depth below the surface; and that a white object sinking into the water turns blue before passing out of sight.

Light cannot penetrate far through seawater and as a result only a little light in the blue area of the spectrum reaches much beyond a depth of 150 feet. Divers who descend into this zone see everything as a blue-grey colour. Below a depth of about 650 feet even this blue light has been absorbed, and so the ocean is almost completely dark ... the few organisms that live at this depth are generally able to generate their own light.

Make yourself comfortable inside your protective Circle and imagine yourself bobbing about on the surface of the sea. On several occasions we have referred to jellyfish ... and this is what you are about to become. Far away from the shore is the environment where they come into their own; here they appear ethereal and graceful. Some give out a brilliant white light, and at night appear as gleaming globes in the water. Although we usually encounter them on the surface, they can descend to great depths.

Begin by relaxing your limbs, and feel your arms and legs becoming lighter, buoyed by the sea. Your whole body begins to take on a weightlessness that enables you to hang in the water, and slowly ... slowly ... you begin to descend in what feels like a slow-motion, flying sensation. You have shape-shifted and developed a body similar to the creature from the Deep in the film *Abyss*, still recognisably human in outline but not of this world.

The water around you has a slightly bluish-green tint, but your body gives off a shimmering, translucent glow so you not in total darkness as you sink lower and lower into the gloom. Remember that your lifeline is that tiny blue light shimmering in the distance, and should you feel 'out of your depth' you only have to head for this blue light and you will return to your Circle ...

You are now suspended in Time and Space, deep in the ocean. You know that Life has its beginnings down here in the Deep ... it is also a descent into the grave. Here you will be in touch with the spiritual forces that built the Universe at the very point of evolving Life. To repeat Eliot's highly appropriate lines:

We must be still and still moving/ Into another intensity/For a further union, a deeper communion/Through the dark cold and the empty desolation ... In the end is my beginning.

No one can say what sensations will come to you in this altered state of consciousness but try not to be afraid: trust your instincts and intuitions. This will be a priceless and unrepeatable moment. You may descend again into the Deep but the sensations will never be the same. When you have had enough, focus on the tiny, shimmering light in the distance and allow your mind to drift slowly upwards to meet it. When you reach the open surface of the sea, clap your hands to dispel any remnants of astral energy, clap your hands and take a hot drink and sweet biscuit to complete the 'earthing' process.

The world of the sea-witch is not confined to the shore and the water margin. It is a multi-dimensional world of light and shadow, of reality and illusion, where we have moved into the subjective world of the spirit – a rich fishing-ground for those who trawl in these inner seas. The Mystery is now within and around us. By immersing ourselves in the world of myth and legend to such a degree, it has become as tangible to us as the 'real' world, forming a continual back-ground to our daily life.

Perhaps this most appropriate of observations from Belgian playwright, poet and essayist, Maurice Polydore Marie Bernard, Count Maeterlinck, provides us with a suitable conclusion to this chapter. Mysticism and metaphysics influenced his writing throughout his career, and he constantly returned to the themes of death and the meaning of life in his works. This extract is from *The Treasure of the Humble*, written in 1896:

> *How strangely do we diminish a thing as soon as we try to express it in words! We believe we have dived down to the most unfathomable depths, and when we reappear on the surface, the drops of water that glistens on our trembling finger-tips no longer represents the sea from which it came. We believe we have discovered a grotto that is stored with bewildering treasure; we come back to the light of day, and the gems we have brought are false – mere pieces of glass – and yet does the treasure shine on, unceasingly in the darkness!*

Classical sea and ocean deities

Oceanus: An ancient Greek deity that represented all the waters that girdle the earth, and from which all springs, rivers and lakes derive. He is depicted as a bearded man, carrying a water-pot or urn. He (saltwater) and his consort Tethys (freshwater), were the primal parents of the gods, and the Oceanids.

Poseidon: In Homer he rates as one of the most powerful gods along with Zeus (lord of heaven) and Hades (lord of the underworld), who sends storms and earthquakes. The horse is his sacred animal and in Corinth, horse-racers were held in his honour. He is often depicted carrying a trident.

Neptune: An old Italian god of flowing water, whose feast was held on 23rd July to ward of the high summer drought. He was equated with Poseidon and identified by the Romans as a god of the sea, and as the patron of race-courses

Nereus: According to Homer, he is 'the Old Man of the Sea' and father of the Nereids. Like all sea-gods he has the gift of prophecy and the ability to shape-shift at will.

Proteus: In the *Odyssey* he is an 'ancient one of the sea' who herds the seals, knows all things, and has the power to shape-shift.

Triton: a Greek sea-god and son of Poseidon, represented with a man head and trunk and a fish's body. He is commonly shown blowing on a conch shell.

Magical tasks and exercises
The journey continues ...

Facing the Ocean
Professor Barry Cunliffe

It is not often that a new idea enters the world of ancient and medieval history, but in *Facing The Ocean*, Barry Cunliffe, Professor of European Archaeology at Oxford, presents a fresh approach that will change our view of our ancestors. After many years of research and fieldwork, he has come to believe that the peoples originating on the Atlantic seaboard, all share an identity shaped by thousands of years of living along the ocean's shore.

Facing The Ocean shows that our shore-living ancestors had a closer kinship with their seafaring neighbours than with their inland countrymen. "Indeed the very act of living on the edge of the world created a collective consciousness that was, and is still today, specifically 'Atlantic' – an identity that has produced cultures of great inventiveness and works of art of beauty and originality."

As part of the next step in our magical quest, this beautifully illustrated book is essential reading for anyone who wishes to understand the rich history that has governed the lives of our island race, together with its myths and legends.

Published by OUP: ISBN 0-19-924019-1: hardback
www.oup.com

Chapter Eight

Sea and Sky

Any spell should begin with the casting of the Circle, so let's take a moment to reflect on what the Circle represents and what it does. Firstly, it is a symbol of 'all things' and an emblem of 'All is One', combining all the various phenomena of the universe and linking them together in Unity. There are many different methods of casting a Circle, but the one most commonly used in this text is the creation of a shimmering blue 'bubble' that wraps itself around the sea-witch – above and below.

Secondly, in magical working, the Circle protects from any negative or hostile intrusion by creating a barrier between this world and Other World. It also acts as a 'holding tank' for the magical energy raised during the Circle working, which is to be harnessed and directed at the matter in hand. If it were not for the Circle, the energy would flow off in all directions and dissipate; the Circle keeps it confined to a small area and concentrates it.

And while we're putting things into perspective, let's also make no bones about it, *spell-casting is an art-form*. Some can do it, others never manage to achieve any results unless they are working with a group of other people. In the *Encyclopaedia of Witches & Witchcraft*, spells are defined 'a spoken or written formula that, in an act of magic, is intended to cause or influence a particular course of events'. It is often said that spell-casting is closely related to prayer, but it is probably more accurate to say it is the product of focusing the Will of the individual by the means of mental imagery; and the raising of personal energy by means of repetitive chanting or movement.

A spell-casting ritual focuses the mind on the image of the

person, animal or 'thing' to be influenced but it is the use of chanting and/or dance that raises the power to achieve the desired result. The secret here is to use a repetitive chant, similar to the one used in the film, *The Craft*, where the would-be witches caused a member of their group to levitate using the refrain: '*Light as a feather, stiff as a board ... light as a feather, stiff as a board ...*'

Yes, it *was* a filmscript but keeping it simple, makes it more powerful because you are not thinking all the time about remembering your lines. If you want to use a full-length charm, then once the whole has been recited during the preparation, take two lines to use as a refrain while you are directing the spell.

List of spells and charms
Charm 9 – The Masque of Queens
A Charm to Bring in the Witch
A Prayer to the Moon Goddess
Spell to Bring Lost Creatures Home
The Binding
Love Spell
Spell for Protection
Good Wishes
Invocation
Banishing
The Tempest
A Spell to Defeat a Rival
Re-directing a Curse

Charm 9 – The Masque of Queens
An example of chanting and dancing being used in spell-casting was this charm written by Ben Jonson for *The Masque of Queens*.

The preparation of the spell is self-explanatory and can be used for all sorts of results but for it to work effectively, it requires the inclusion of repetitive dancing (or pacing) and chanting. If several people are taking part then it can be used as part of the Circle dance to raise the power. A solitary practitioner should recite the whole while preparing the charm and then use two or three lines as a refrain, i.e. *'Around, around, Till a music sound, And the pace be found ...'*

About, about and about,
Till the mist arise and the lights fly out;
The images neither be seen not felt;
The woolen burn and the waxen melt;
Sprinkle your liquors upon the ground
And into the air, around, around.
   Around, around,
   Around, around,
   Till a music sound
   And the pace be found
   To which we may dance
   And our charms advance

The Masque of Queens was performed at Whitehall on 2nd February 1609 for the entertainment of the Court, the details of which were taken from supposed 'confessions' of the time.

A Charm to Bring in the Witch

A Charm to Bring in the Witch was written by Robert Herrick and could be used against someone instigating a psychic attack.

To house the Hag, you must doe this;
Commix with Meade a little Pisse
Of him bewitcht: then forthwith make
A little Wafer or a Cake;
And this rawly bak't will bring
The old Hag in. No surer thing.

Urine was (and still is) a powerful ingredient in magical preparation and a true witch will not shy away from using it. Here, it is used as part of the charm to deflect 'bewitchment' or psychic attack by 'bottling' the sender's energies.

For added protection and also to act as a 'binding' spell on the perpetrator, it would be a good idea to place the wafer or cake inside a small glass bottle or jar that can be sealed tight. Keep the jar in a place of discomfort, i.e. the freezer, in the coal shed, outside lavatory, etc. If the victim feels further twinges of discomfort, he or she should shake the jar vigorously in order to upset the equilibrium of the sender.

Robert Herrick was an English lyric poet [1591-1674] unrivalled in his field and author of the popular *Gather ye Rose Buds, Cherry Ripe, Oberon's Feast*, etc. Many of his works referred to witchcraft.

A Prayer to the Moon Goddess (Divination)

"A large amount of folk-lore was passed down to children in the form of rhymes to make it more easily remembered. Many of these were regarded as children's entertainment and accordingly have found their way into a body of work we now refer generally as 'Mother Goose'." [*Earth, Air, Fire, Water*]

Luna, every woman's friend,
To me they goodness condescend,
Let this night in visions see
Emblems of my destiny.

It is interesting that this particular rhyme doesn't ask for a romantic image to be shown, which was the thinly veiled excuse for using spell-casting under the guise of superstition and harmless fun. British folk-lore in full of rhymes and charms to help girls see or find a lover or husband, but if we look behind the veil of illusion, we can often see the original intent.

As with all forms of divination, the results are more than likely to be in the form of symbols (or emblems) that need to be interpreted and may not be instantly recognisable. Results of this nature should be recorded in a magical journal for future reference.

Spell to Bring Lost Creatures Home

This *Spell to Bring Lost Creatures Home* was written in the early part of the 20th century by Kathleen Raine and is a long poem from which this short extract will be useful for the sea-witch.

Home, home,
Wanderers home,
Cormorant to rock,
Gulls from the storm
Boat to the harbour
Safe sail home!

If a storm is brewing then this simple spell can be recited over and over again, adding any further lines you choose.

The Binding

The Binding is an adaptation from a Robert Herrick poem and although it can be used for lovers, it can also be utilised to bind an enemy by using horse-hair for added strength.

'Tis but silke that bindeth thee,
Knap the thread, and thou are free:
But 'tis otherwise with me;
You are bound, and fast bound so,
That from me you cannot go.

It was thought that witches could cause storms, raise tempests and generally wreak havoc with the weather by letting their hair flow loosely. In 17th century Scotland, this was still a popular superstition and local women were prevented from combing their hair while their brothers were away at sea.

Lovers often exchanged locks of hair as proof of devotion, for the simple reason that if one betrayed the other, the hair could be used in a spell against the unfaithful lover. It was also a belief that a woman was rendered powerless if she had no hair and it was for this reason that the Inquisitors shaved the heads of witches before torturing them.

Love Spell

Another early 20th century poem from Kathleen Raine was *Love Spell* from which this is an extract pertinent to the sea-witch …

> *By the foam of the surf*
> *By the curve of the wave*
> *By the flowing of the tide,*
>
> *By the way of the sun,*
> *By the dazzle of light*
> *By the path across the sea*
>   *Bring my lover*
>
> *By the cormorant's cliff*
> *By the seal's rock*
> *By the raven's crag,*
>
> *By the shells on the strand*
> *By the ripples on the sand*
> *By the brown sea-wrack*
>   *Bring my lover*

Although this is a standard love spell, lines seven and fourteen could easily convert to other 'demands' – such as a request for information, wealth, etc. Ideally it should be performed at the water's edge, using the 'path of light' created by the setting sun.

Spell for Protection

This Spell for Protection is an extract from a longer version by Jeni Couzyn included in *Earth, Air, Fire, Water* ...

By cool blood of fish
By gill and fin
By scale and skeleton
Let no harm come to ....

Everyone at some time or another, needs to place a magical seal of protection around their home and its occupants. In fact, a sea-witch, like her inshore cousins should ensure that this is renewed every few months.

This simple protection rite would ideally be accompanied by the offering of a fish – either caught for the purpose of the rite or purchased from a fishmonger. Those who live and work on the sea have no qualms in catching and killing fish, but not everyone is up to the task, and so a shop-bought fish will suffice.

Take the fish down to the seashore and recite the above verse as you throw it into the water. The fish is a traditional creature of sacrifice and if the petitioner lives inland a tin of sardines or pilchards offered to the neighbouring cat will do as a substitute.

Good Wishes

Good Wishes came from an anonymous poem and different wording to express the same sentiments can be found all over the country, often being adapted to suit the type of landscape or environment.

Bounty of sea be thine
Bounty of land be thine

Such good wishes can be used to sign a letter or greetings card; as a toast to someone's health or good fortune; as a greeting or as a means of saying goodbye. There are many such sayings used in Craft and this one would be suitable for a sea-witch and her companions.

Invocation

Fragment is an anonymous invocation that could be used as part of a sea-witch's ritual ...

> *As it was,*
> *As it is,*
> *As it shall be*
> *Evermore,*
> *O Thou Triune*
> *Of grace!*
> *With the ebb*
> *With the flow,*
> *O Thou Triune*
> *Of grace!*
> *With the ebb*
> *With the flow*

Here the word 'triune' probably comes from the Latin *trium*, meaning a third part or a third of anything, and can either refer to the triple aspect of the goddess in contemporary Wicca; or the triple imagery of earth, sea and sky.

In magical or mystical terms, the number three has many connotations, and almost every nation has regarded this number as sacred. The occult symbol is the figure of the Empress, and the Tarot representation generally depicts a crowned woman holding in her hand the orb of the world. It is imbued with the highest wisdom and harmony, perfect love, soul force, brilliant action and tenderness. It bestows plenty, fruitfulness, and the power for important exertion. For the sea-witch, this invocation would be highly appropriate.

Banishing

There comes a time when every witch will need to carry out a *Banishing* or cleansing rite and basically any form of words can be used. Witches, as we have seen, tend to prefer a simple jingle like the following, using salt, water and incense.

Method:
Take a small amount of Maldon salt and cast it into a bowl of fresh water as you recite the formula for banishing ...

Water and earth
Where you are cast
No spell nor adverse purpose last
Not in complete accord with me.
As my word, so mote it be!

Sprinkle the now consecrated water around the area that needs cleansing and then throw a small amount of loose incense into the burner saying ...

Creatures of fire and air
This charge I lay,
No phantom in thy presence stay.
Here my will addressed to thee;
And as my word, so mote it be!

The smoke from the incense should then be allowed to roll around the area that needs cleansing.

The important thing about this rite is that you *must* focus all your Will into dismissing all and any negative energy that may be lurking around. The point of the exercise is to impose your magical Will on any unwelcome entity that may have manifested in the area.

The Tempest

In William Shakespeare's *The Tempest*, there are a couple of sonnets that have been put to music by a variety of contemporary performers. Known as 'Ariel's Song', both parts can be used for magical working and if the recorded versions can be obtained, these can be utilised as background music for your rites.

Come unto these yellow sands,
And then take hands;
Court'sied when you have, and kiss'd,
(The wild waves whist,)
Foot it featly here and there;
And, sweet sprites, the burden bear.
Hark, hark!
The watch-dogs bark:
Hark, hark, I hear
The strain of strutting chanticleer,
Cry, Cock-a-doodle-doo.

Full fathom five thy father lies;
Of his bones are coral made;
These are pearls that were his eyes;
Nothing of him that doth fade,
But doth suffer a sea-change
Into something rich and strange.
Sea-nymphs hourly ring his knell:
Hark! Now I hear them—ding-dong, bell.

A Spell to Defeat a Rival

On a small, clean piece of paper draw a figure of eight, like a Mobius Strip; in one half write your lover's name and your rival's name in the other half. Cut the 8 in half and, holding your rival's half over a flame, recite the following as it burns ...

Bring all the thief has taken, back to our house
Bring all the thief has taken, back to our bed
Bring all the thief has taken, back to our love
Bring all the thief has taken, back to me

Collect up all the ash and take it outside. Throwing it into the air, say:

Let the wind take you
Let the water take you
Let the rain take you.

You are but a burr in his sock
You are but a grain in his shoe
Now he will forget you.

Keep the half with your lover's name in a safe place amongst your personal possessions – and wait for the spell to take. It is often said that spells should never be cast in anger but the energy generated by anger will help speed it on its way. The more impassioned the delivery, the stronger the spell will grow.

This spell can also be adapted for other reasons, i.e. a rival in business, who has used underhand means to entice your customers away, or someone taking away your good name by gossip and innuendo.

Re-directing a Curse

Re-channelling or re-directing a curse is the only way to get rid of it, for once placed, it cannot be lifted … but it *can* be returned to its sender!

Ideally, this required something from the person *placing* the curse (hair, nail pairings, saliva, etc., anything in fact that contains that person's DNA). Failing that, a picture or photograph will do. Write the name of the sender on a piece of paper and then burn it in a metal container, with these words:

Three blows hast thou dealt;
By evil heart, evil eye and evil tongue.
These same three blows be thine own reward!
By fire and water, earth and air,
And that which binds and governs them
I charge thee, touch him/her not!

Unfortunately, it seems to be highly fashionable these days for folk to claim they are being magically attacked when, in fact, their troubles are a result of their own negative attitude to life. They also prefer to let other people work a counter-charm on their behalf, rather than attempting to carry out the work themselves.

Should you find yourself in this position, stop and ask yourself why the person involved isn't attempting to resolve his or her own problems. Are they really under some form of magical or psychic attack? Or are they merely attracting negative energies because of a lack of moral fibre? Is the alleged attack actually a return of something they themselves have sent out previously?

Never rush in to carry out any form of cleansing or banishment until you are in full possession of the facts – or things just might rebound on you!

Hopefully, *Traditional Witchcraft for the Seashore* demonstrates, that there is an advantage to working on the seashore than merely living in an attractive environment. The next time you visit the coast, take the time to 'stand and stare', and to look at the sea with a new pair of eyes.

Author Biography

Writing as Mélusine Draco, the author has been a magical and spiritual instructor for over 20 years, and writer of numerous popular books including *Liber Agyptius: the Book of Egyptian Magic; The Egyptian Book of Days; The Egyptian Book of Nights; The Thelemic Handbook; The Hollow Tree,* an elementary guide to the Qabalah; *A Witch's Treasury of the Countryside; Root & Branch: British Magical Tree Lore* and *Starchild,* a rediscovery of stellar wisdom. Her highly individualistic teaching methods and writing draws on ancient sources, supported by academic texts and current archaeological findings. The latest titles, *Dictionary of Magic and Mystery, Traditional Witchcraft for Urban Living* and *Traditional Witchcraft for the Seashore* will be published by Moon Books in 2012.

Sources and Bibliography

Book of the British Countryside (Drive Publications)

Britain BC, Francis Pryor (Harper Collins)

British Wild Flowers, W J Stokoe (Warne)

Countryside, Geoffrey Grigson (Ebury)

Earth, Ed: James F Luhr (DK)

Earth, Air, Fire, Water, Robert Skelton & Margaret Blackwood (Arkana)

Earth Story, Simon Lamb and David Sington (BBC)

Facing the Ocean, Barry Cunliffe (OUP)

Folk-lore, Myths & Customs of Britain, Marc Alexander (Sutton)

Folk-lore, Myths & Legends of Britain, (Reader's Digest)

Four Elements, Rebecca Rupp (Profile)

Geology & Scenery in England & Wales, A E Trueman (Pelican)

The History of the Kings of Britain, Geoffrey of Monmouth (Folio)

Old Time Herbs for Northern Gardens, Minnie Watson Kamm (Dover)

The Oxford Book of English Verse (OUP)

The Pebbles on the Beach, Clarence Ellis (Faber)

The Penguin Guide to Superstitions of Britain & Ireland, Steve Roud (Penguin)

Practical Yacht Navigator, Kenneth Wilkes (Nautical)

Really Small Gardens, Jill Billington (RHS)

Seas & Islands, Keith Hiscock (Reader's Digest)

Sea Priestess, Dion Fortune (Aquarian)

Sea & Seashore, I O Evans, (Warne)

Sea Witch, Paul Holman (ignotus)

Secrets of the Seashore (Reader's Digest)

Supernature, Lyall Watson (Coronet)

The Way of the Sea, Timothy Freke, (David & Charles)

Weather, Gerald M. Lester (Warne)

Weatherwise, Paul John Goldsack (David & Charles

Wild Flowers of Britain, Roger Phillips (Pan)

BOOKS

O is a symbol of the world, of oneness and unity. In different cultures it also means the "eye," symbolizing knowledge and insight. We aim to publish books that are accessible, constructive and that challenge accepted opinion, both that of academia and the "moral majority."

Our books are available in all good English language bookstores worldwide. If you don't see the book on the shelves ask the bookstore to order it for you, quoting the ISBN number and title. Alternatively you can order online (all major online retail sites carry our titles) or contact the distributor in the relevant country, listed on the copyright page.

See our website **www.o-books.net** for a full list of over 500 titles, growing by 100 a year.

And tune in to myspiritradio.com for our book review radio show, hosted by June-Elleni Laine, where you can listen to the authors discussing their books.

mySpiritRadio